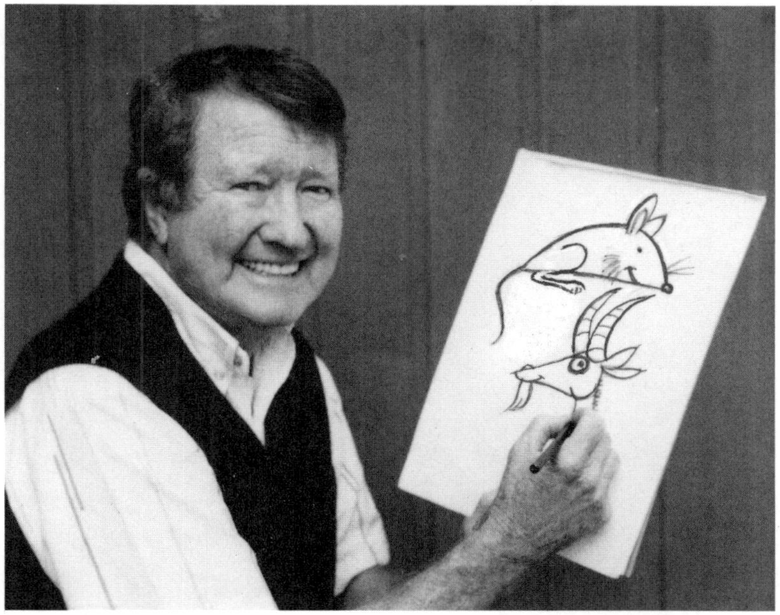

Bud Shackelford, formerly with Walt Disney, is a nationally known artist and teacher. He is listed in "WHO'S WHO IN AMERICAN ART". Shackelford has utilized drawing throughout his professional career as an illustrator, art director, and watercolorist, now concentrating on animal and wildlife subjects. "A good foundation in drawing is important for any art career," states Shackelford, "and the ability to draw well is one of the real pleasures in life."

Bud has delighted children from California to Florida with his humorous way of looking for the basic shapes in every animal and putting this skill on paper. He learned that straightforward approach during the invaluable education he received at the Disney Studios. Large herds of animals of all size and ages were brought to the sound stage, where top instructors worked with the artists to capture on paper the shapes of the moving animals.

"Uncle Bud", as he is affectionately known to children, hopes to reach and inspire many more young artists with this book.

Published by Bud Shackelford
11532 Rolling Hills Dr.
El Cajon, California 92020

Printed in the U.S.A.
Library of Congress Card Number 92-096937
ISBN 0-9634693-0-4

FOR CHILDREN, PARENTS & TEACHERS

This book makes it easy to draw animals, starting with a simple shape, which is the basis for all good drawing. All school children are familiar with circles, squares, rectangles, triangles, and ovals. Variations of these shapes are found in all subjects in nature, and have been utilized by artists throughout history.

The young artist can use sheets of paper or a paper pad, and soft pencil or other drawing instrument. He then starts with the simple shape (shown in red) and continues to complete steps 2, 3, and 4 over his basic shape.

The first drawings are simple and easy. As the student progresses, the drawings are more advanced, and more challenging. Results will be very rewarding.

Owl

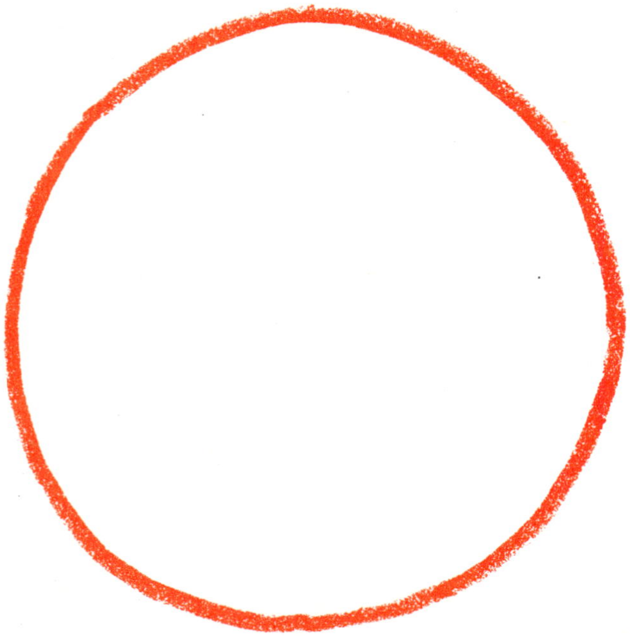

1. Draw a circle.

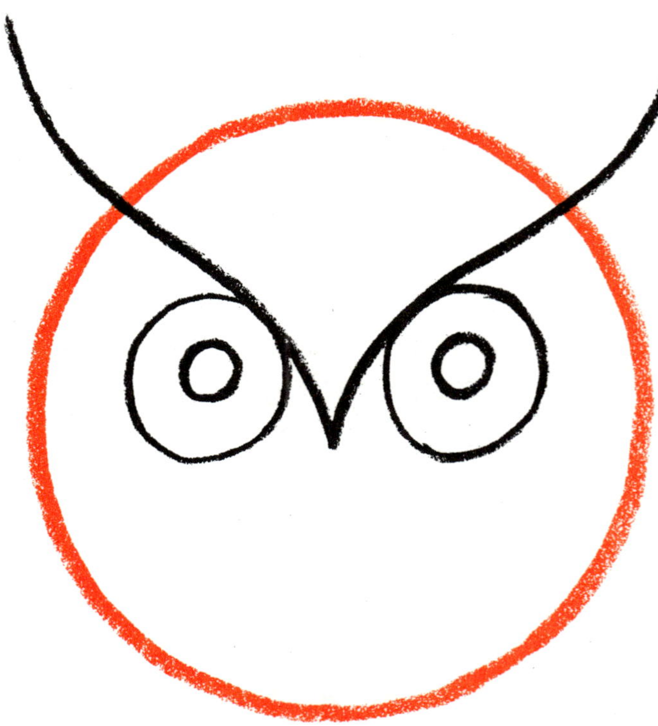

2. Draw more circles for eyes, and two curved shapes from eyebrows to ears.

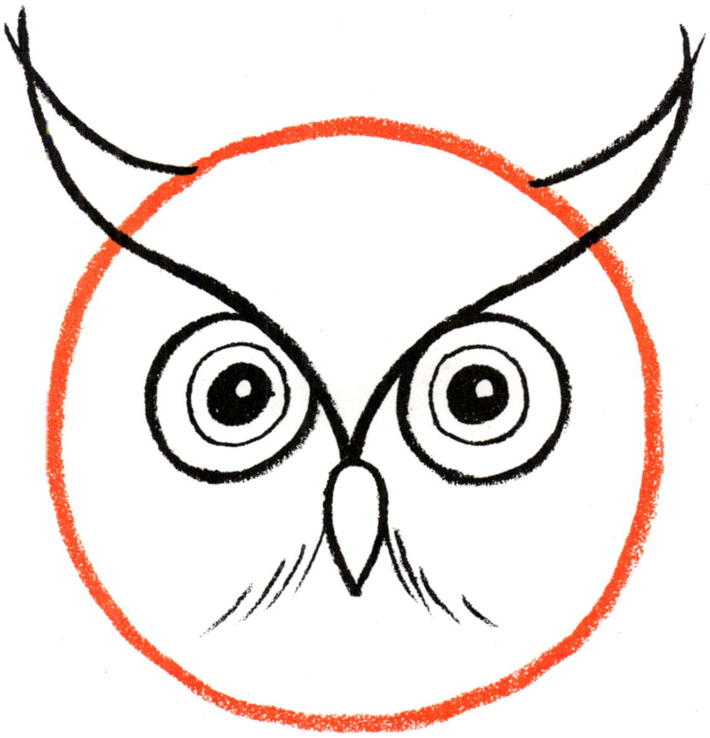

3. Finish ears and eyes.
Add beak and cheeks.

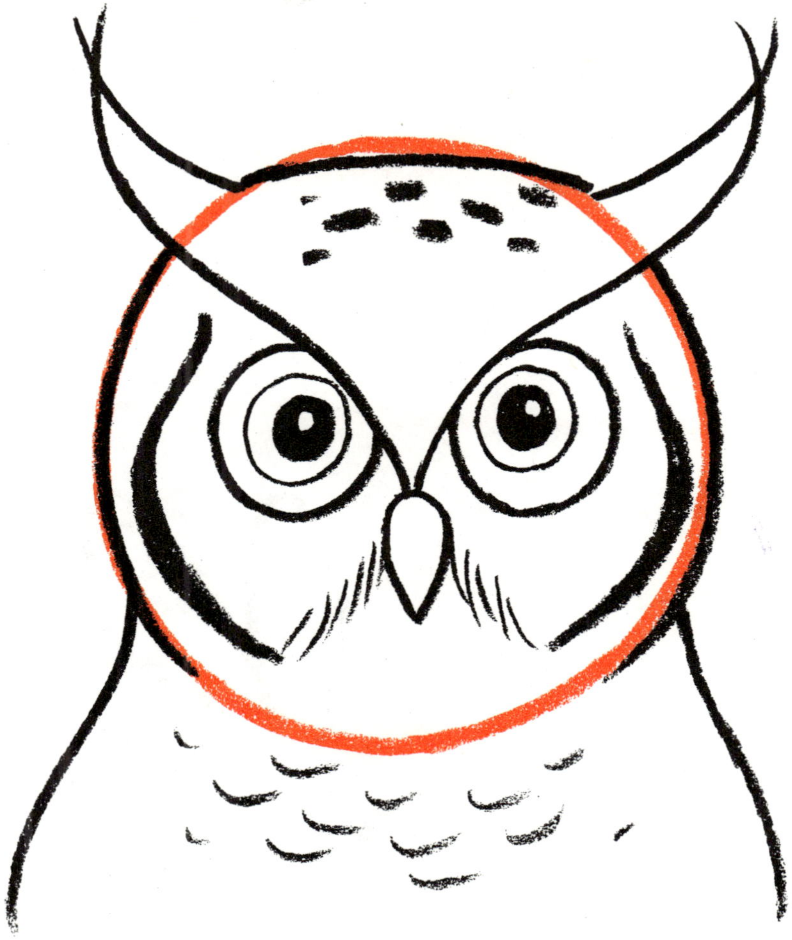

4. Complete markings as shown.
Add shoulders.

Mouse

1. Start with a long dome shape.

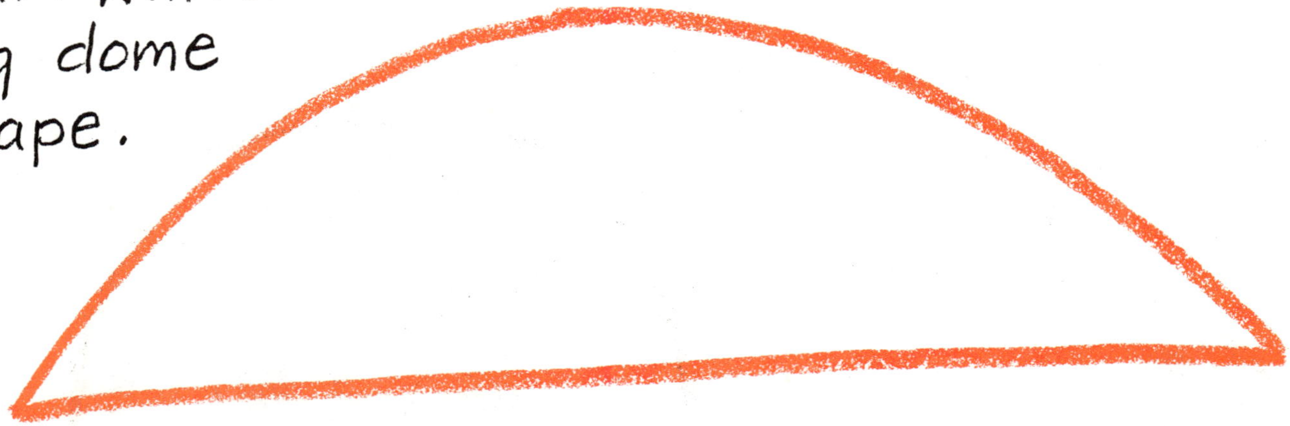

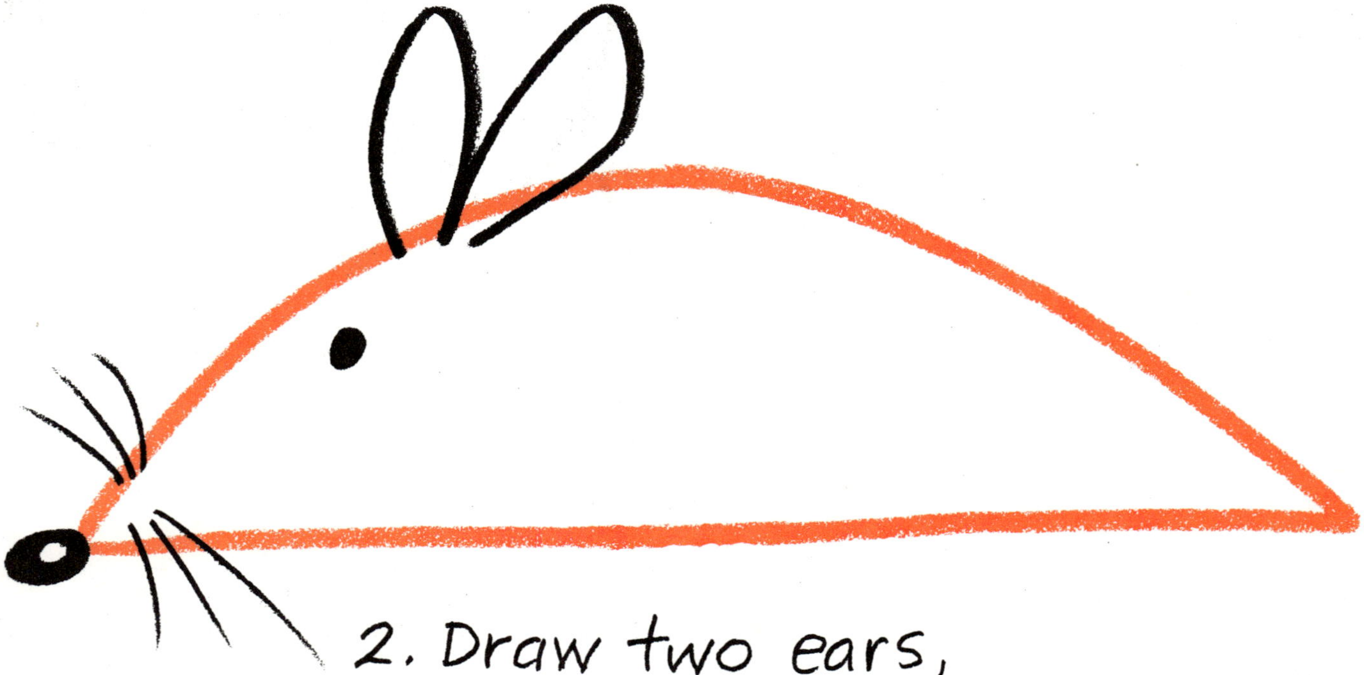

2. Draw two ears, a tiny dot eye, a nose and whiskers.

3. Add tiny running feet...

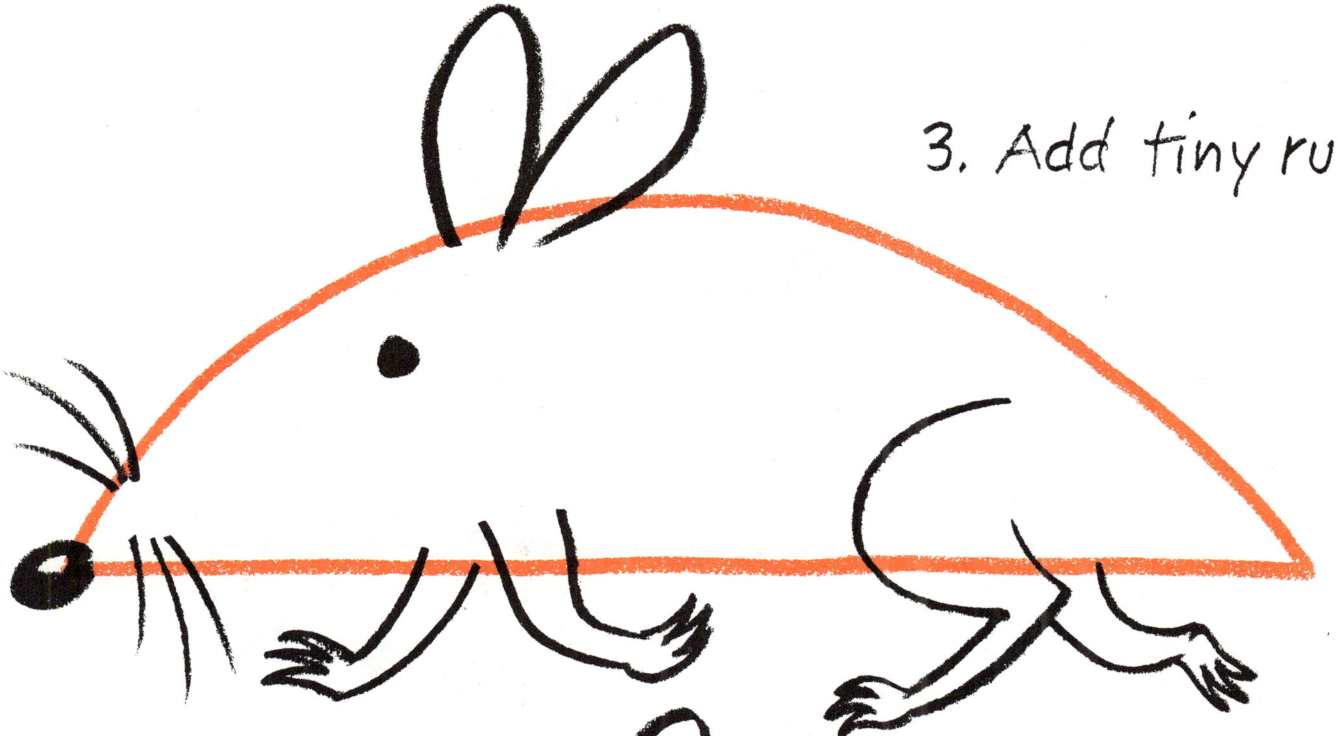

4. a bristly hairy jaw...

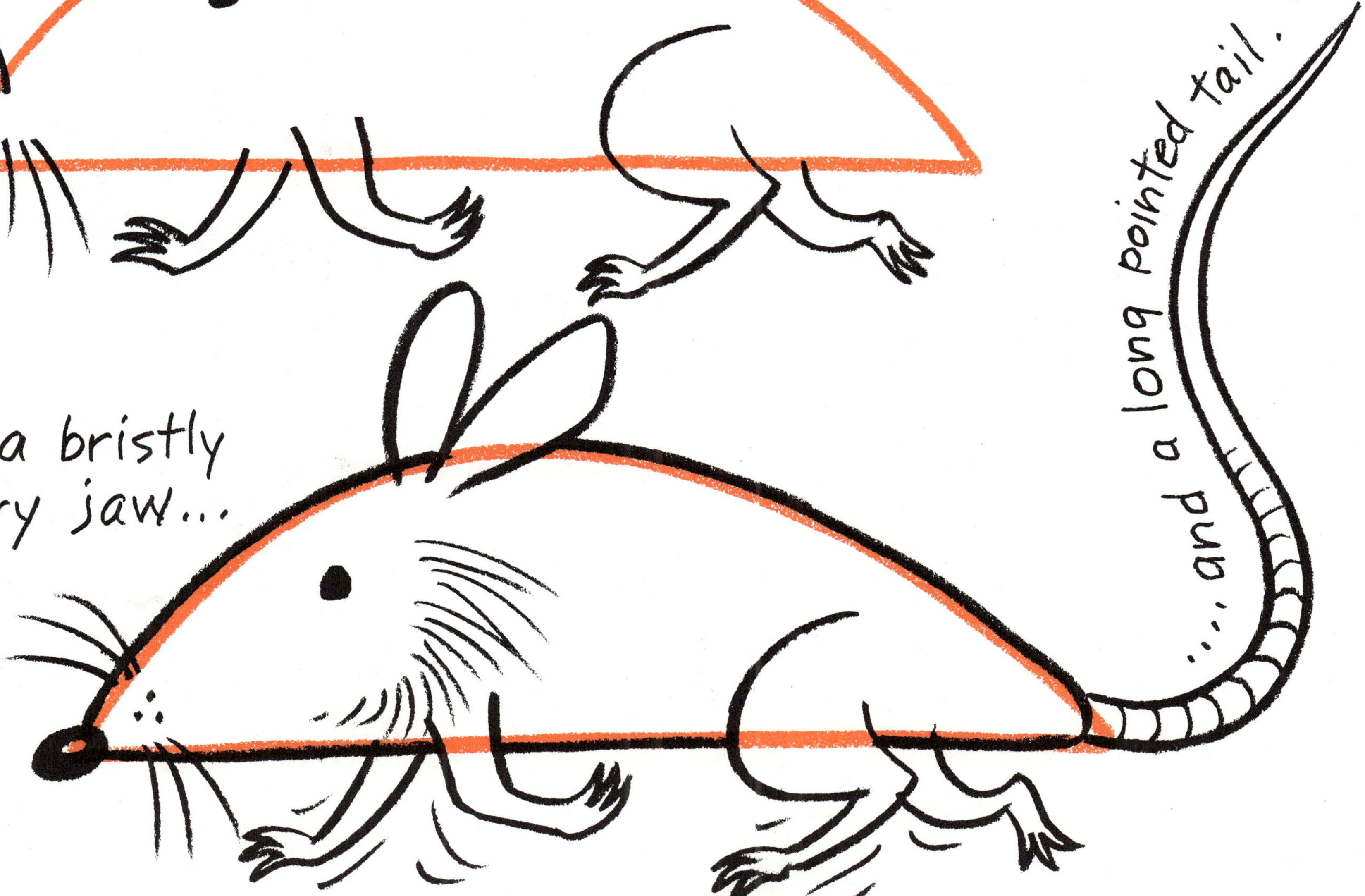

...and a long pointed tail.

Crab

1. Draw a square.

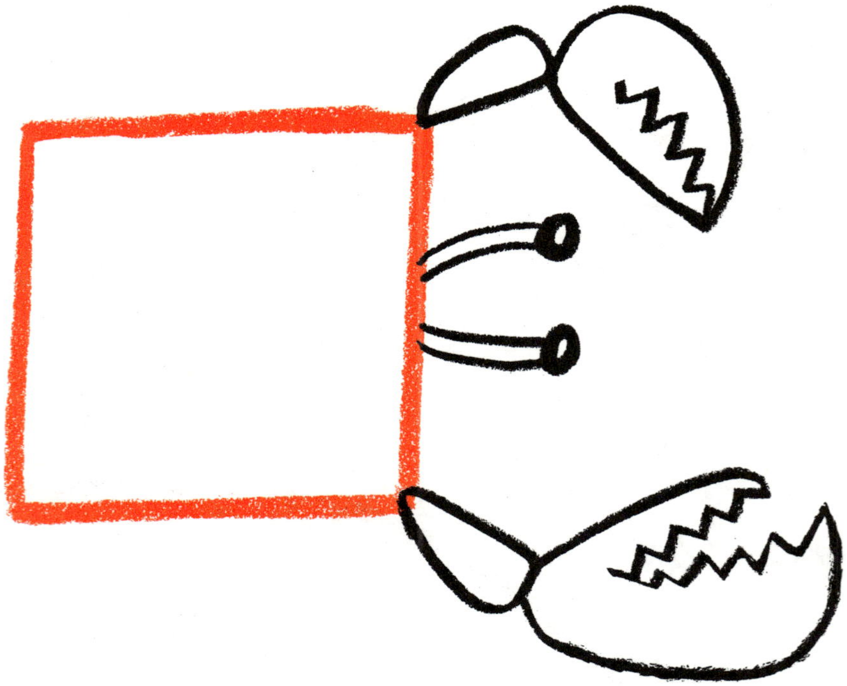

2. Add two eyes and two claws.

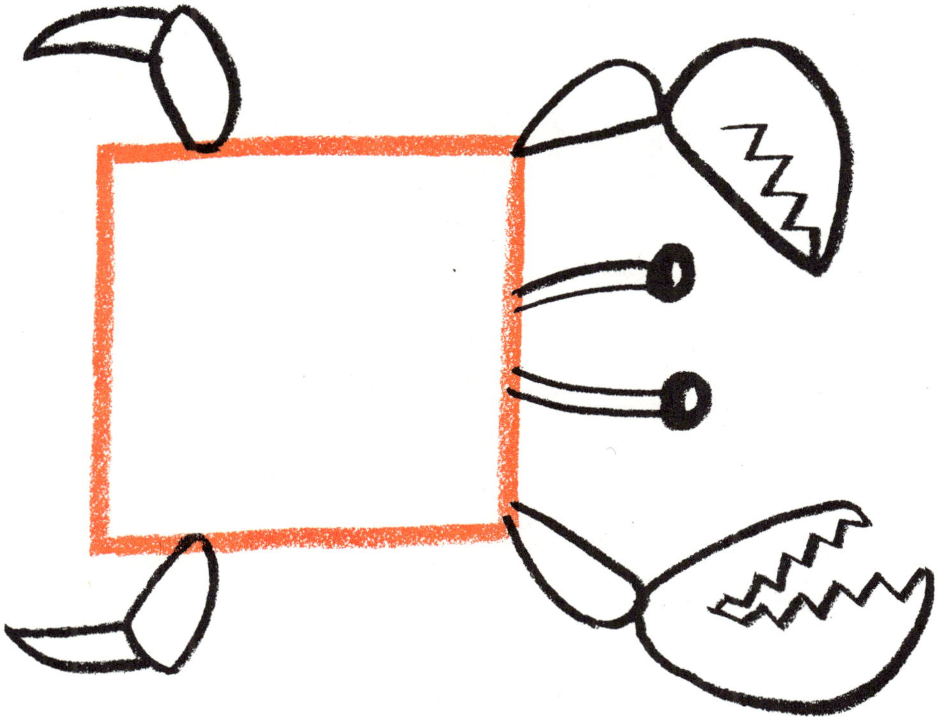

3. Draw two thick rear legs.

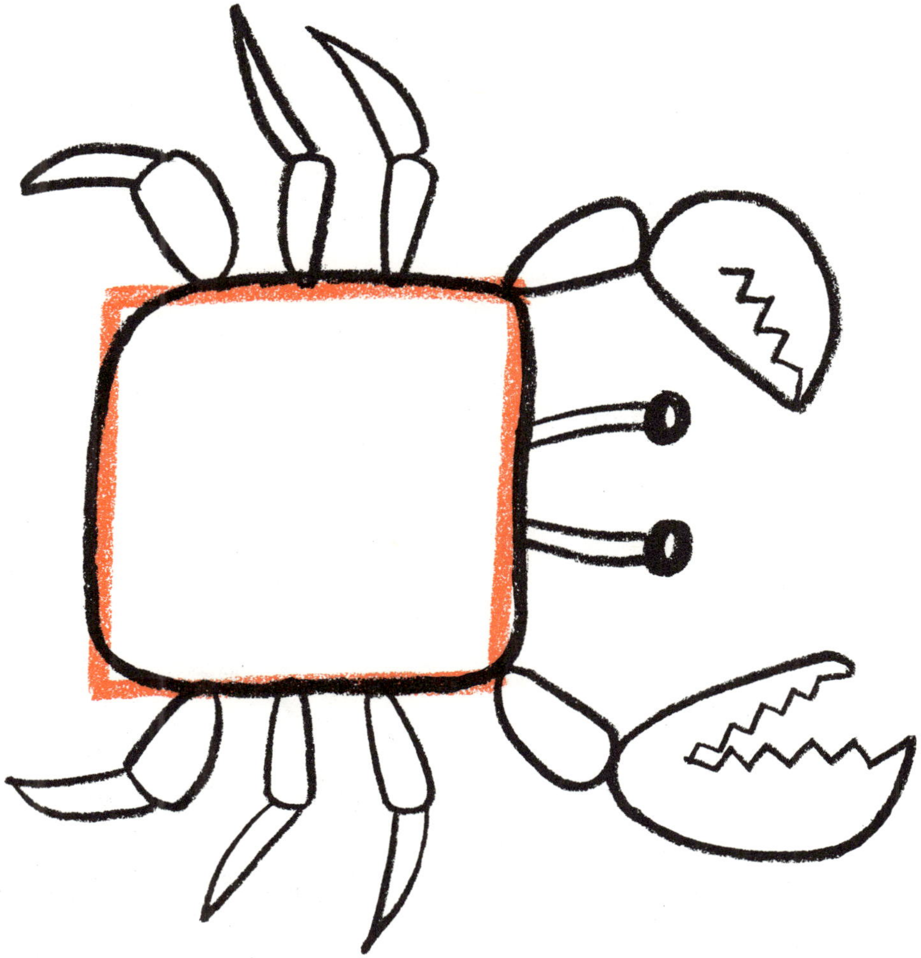

4. Finish with two thinner legs on each side, and round off the corners of the shell.

Turtle

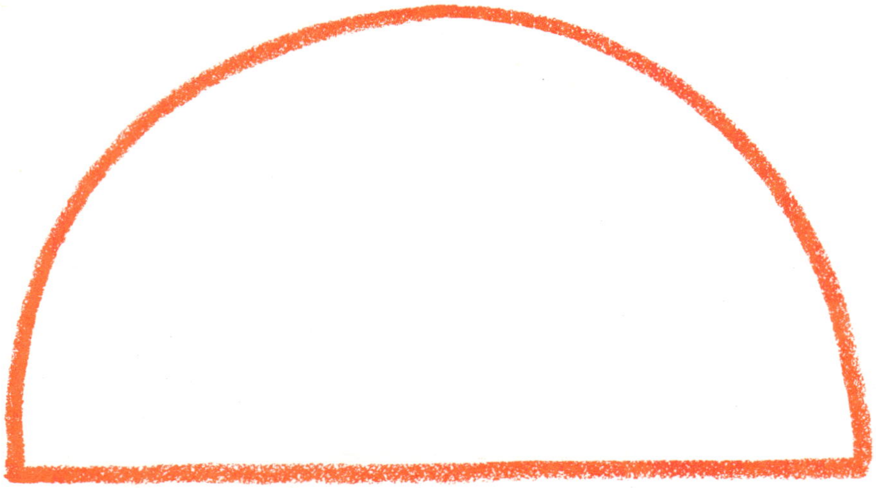

1. Draw a half circle.

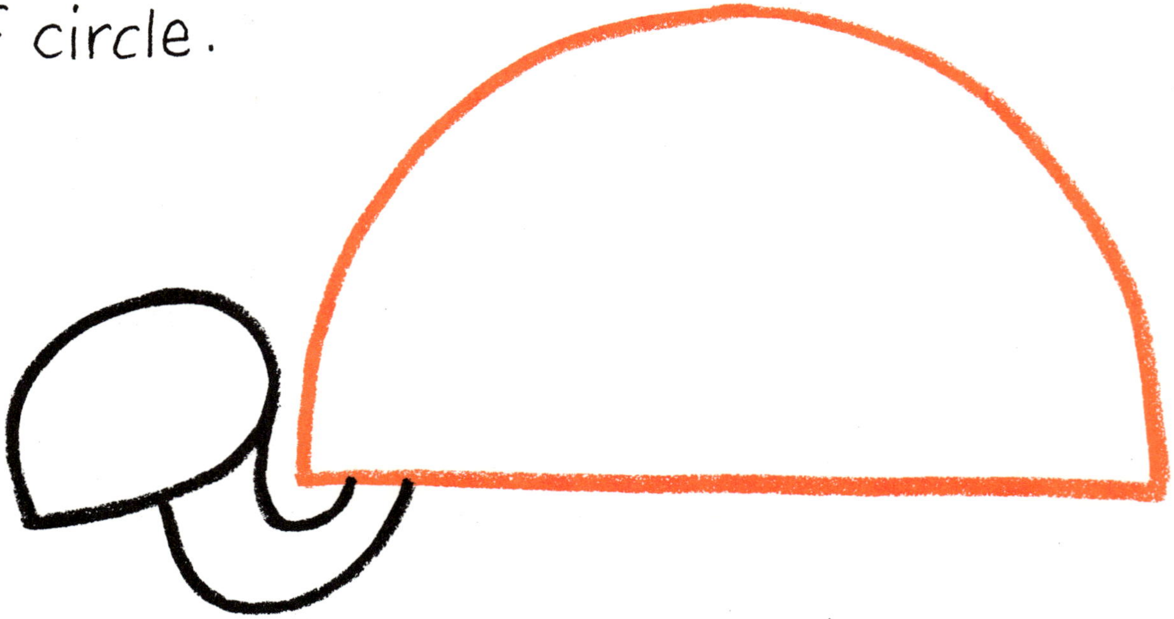

2. Add a head and neck.

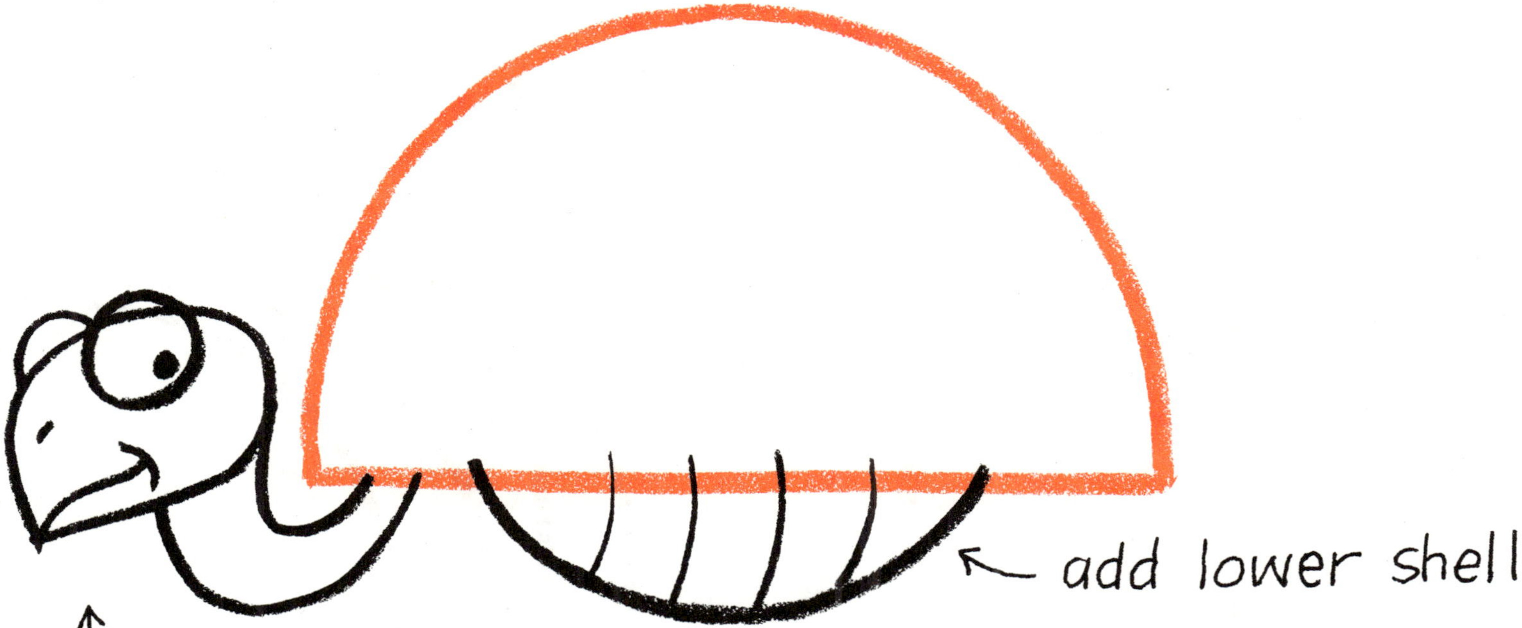

3. Draw eyes and mouth.

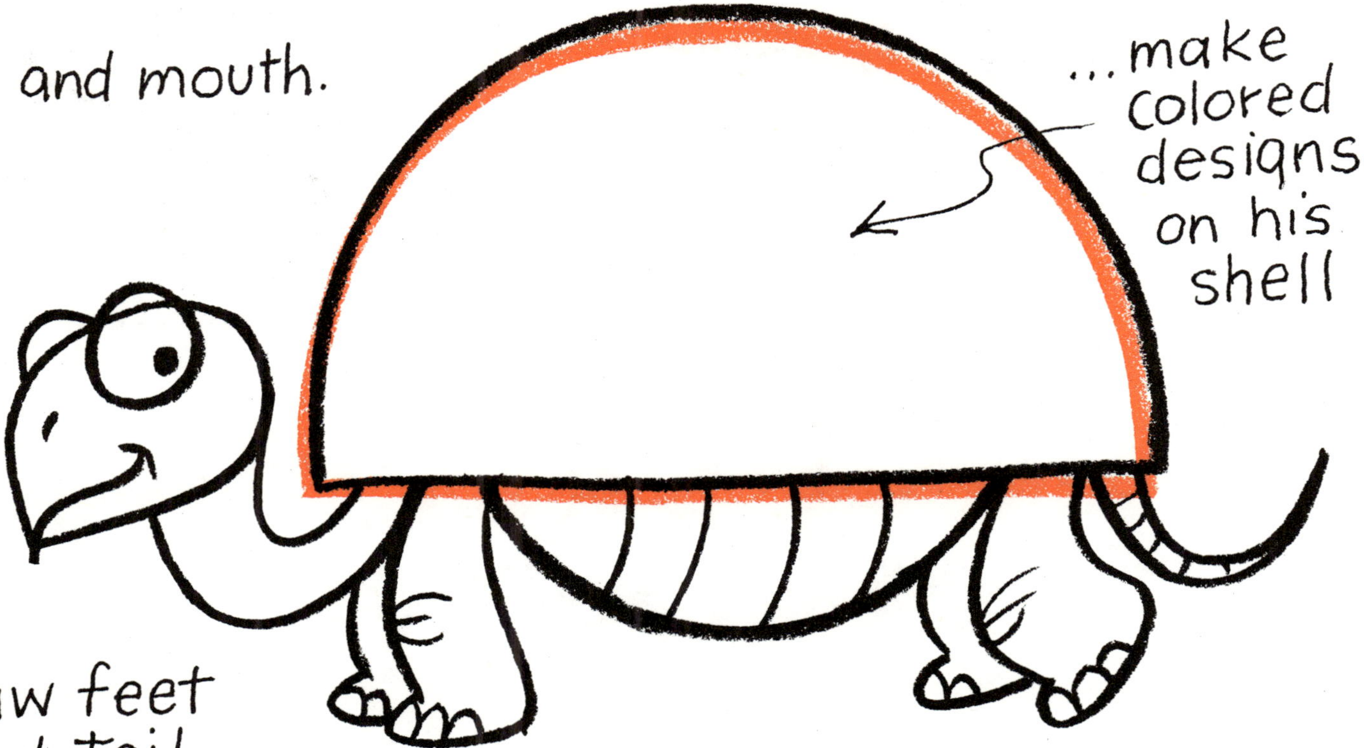

4. Draw feet and tail.

Goat

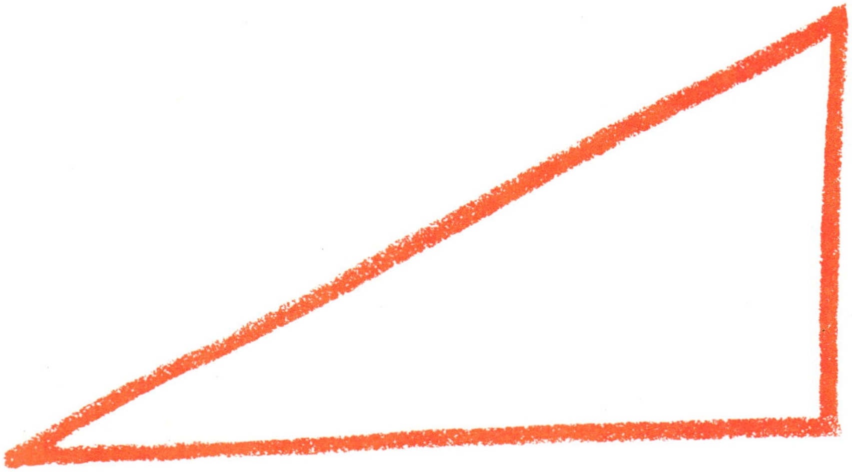

1. Draw a long triangle.

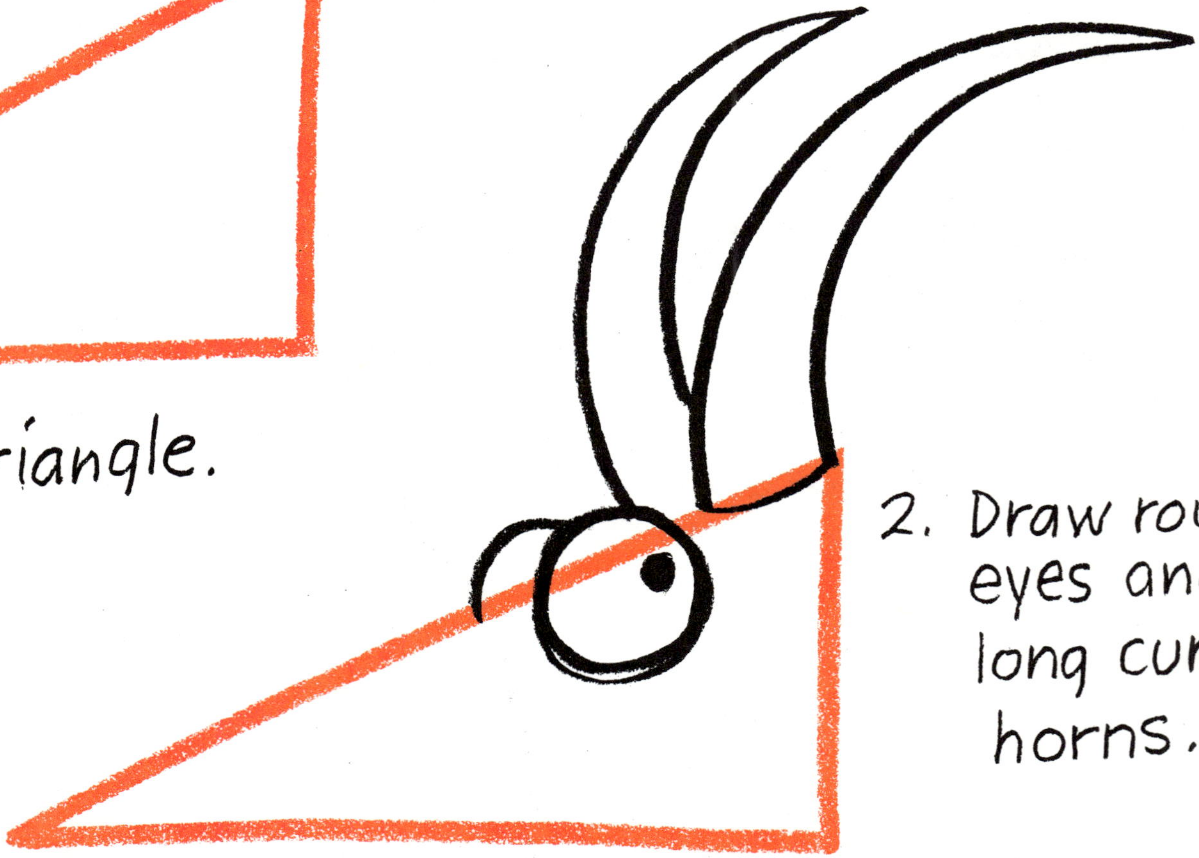

2. Draw round eyes and long curved horns.

3. Add nostril and mouth with a flowing beard.

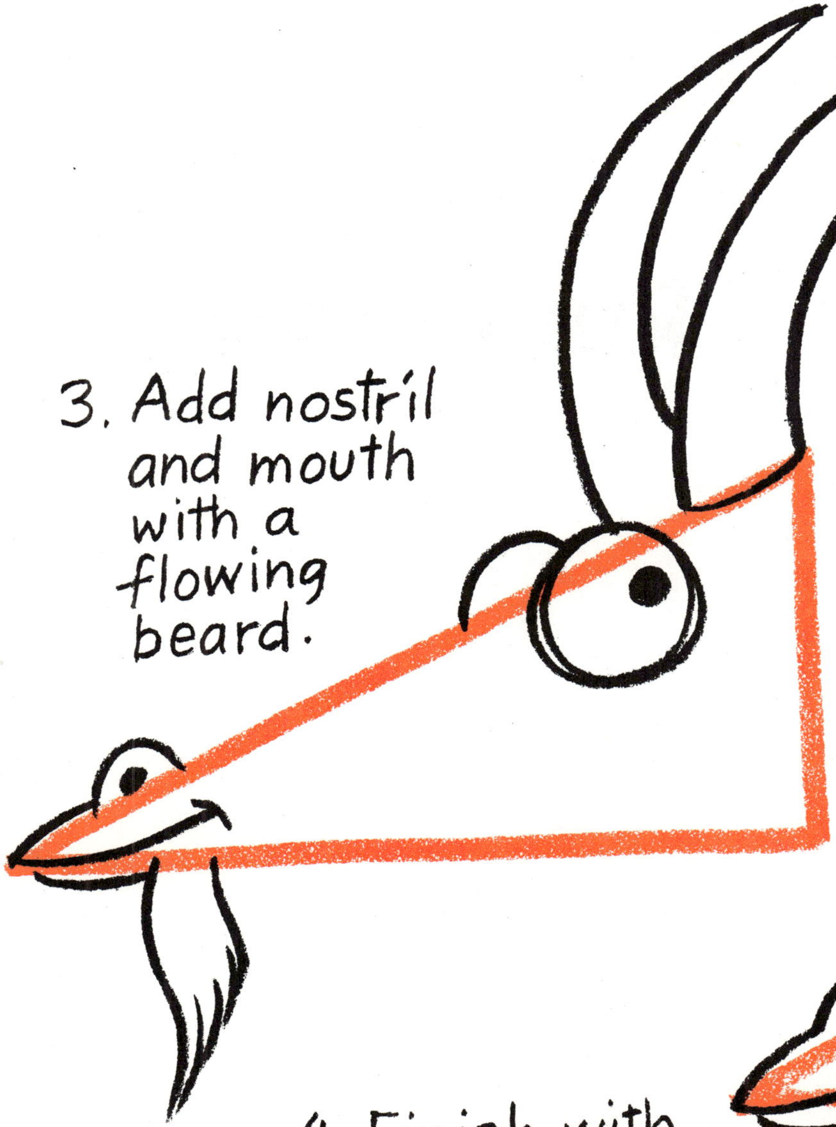

4. Finish with two ears...

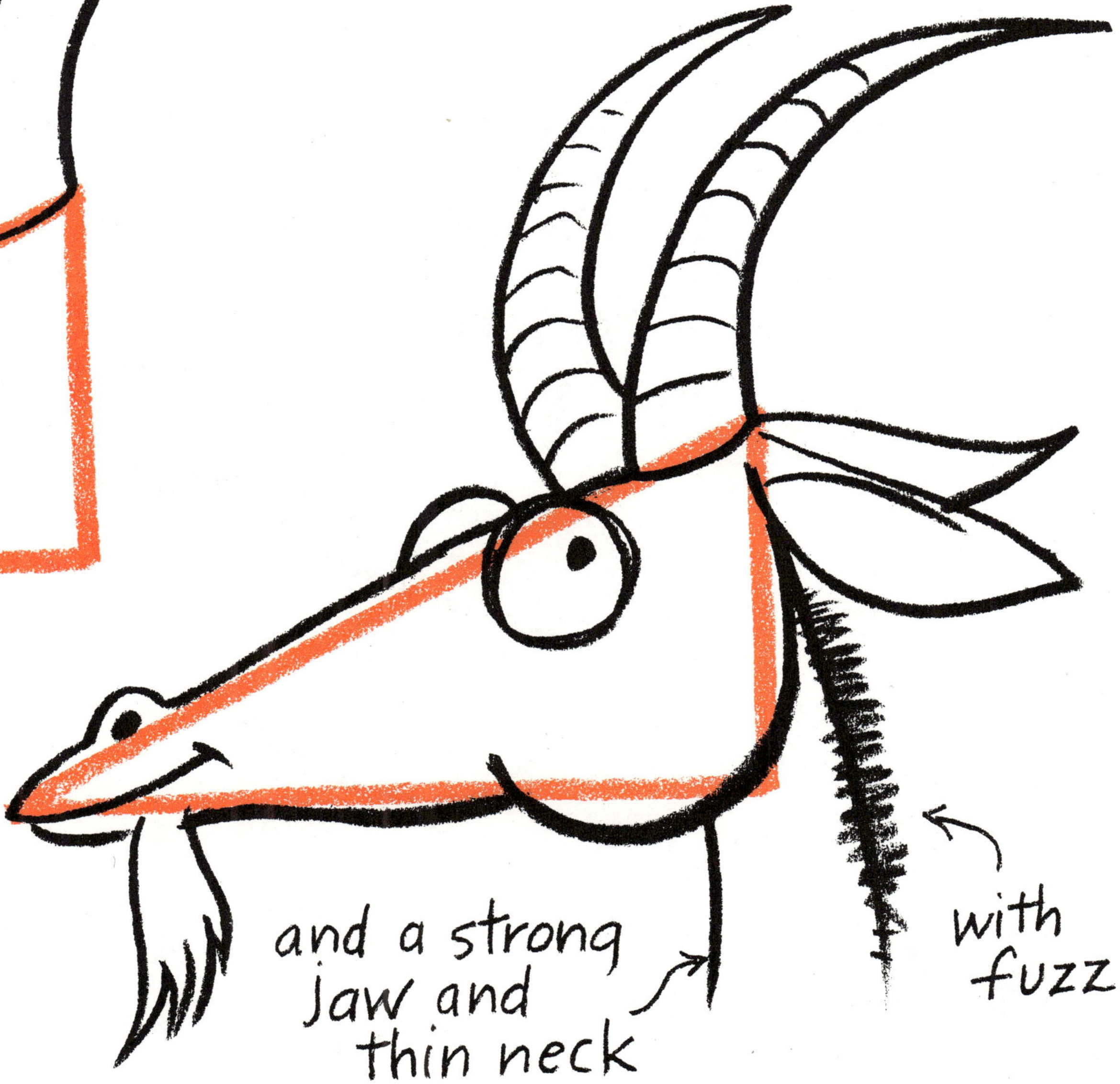

and a strong jaw and thin neck

with fuzz.

Rhinoceros

1. Draw a rectangle.

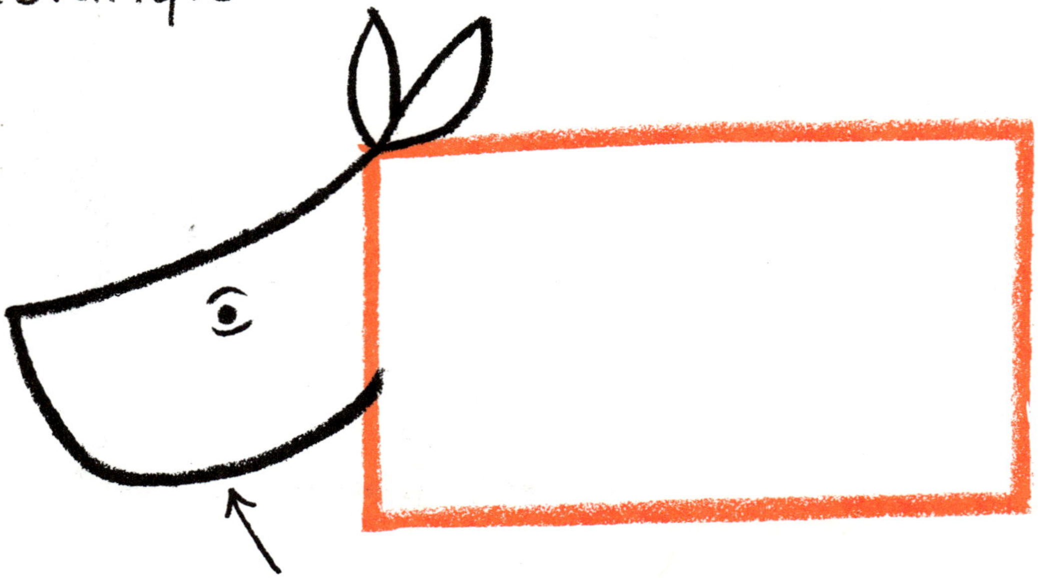

2. Add a long sagging head shape, an eye and two ears.

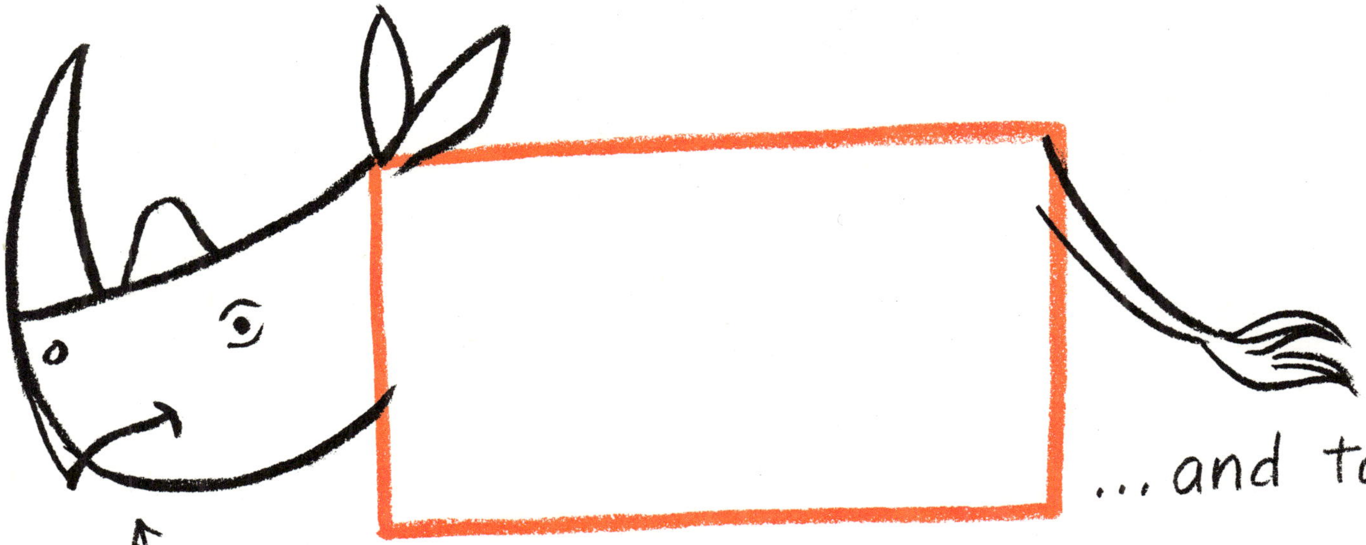

...and tail.

3. Draw two horns, a mouth, lip and nostril...

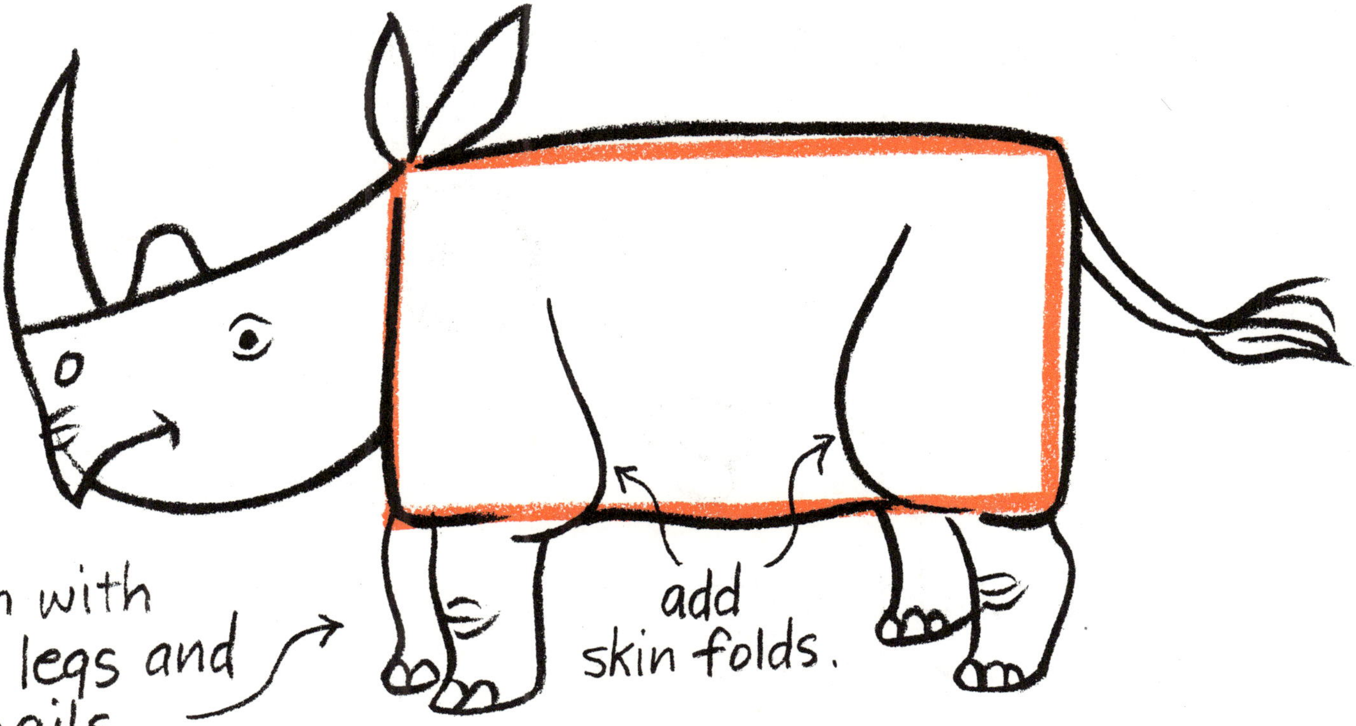

4. Finish with short legs and toenails.

Fish

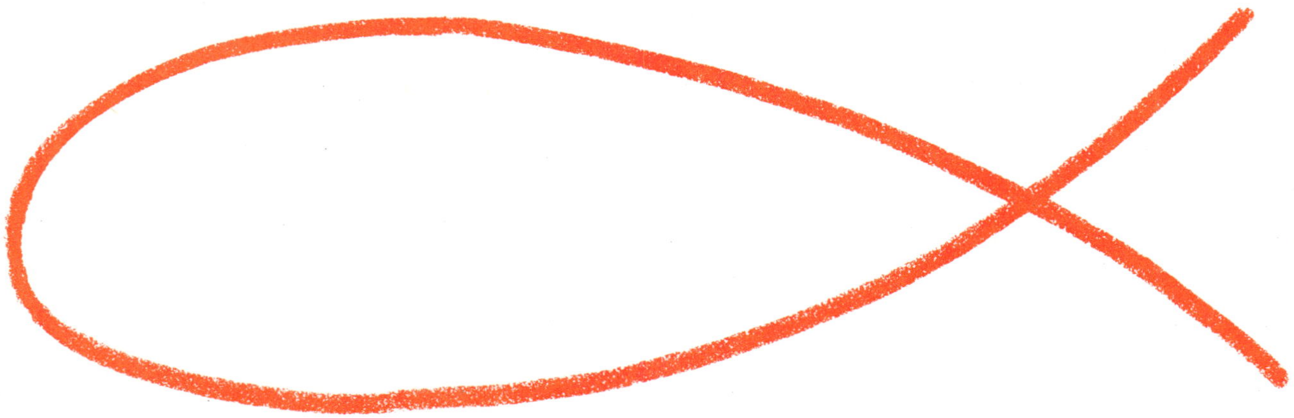

1. Draw an extended teardrop.

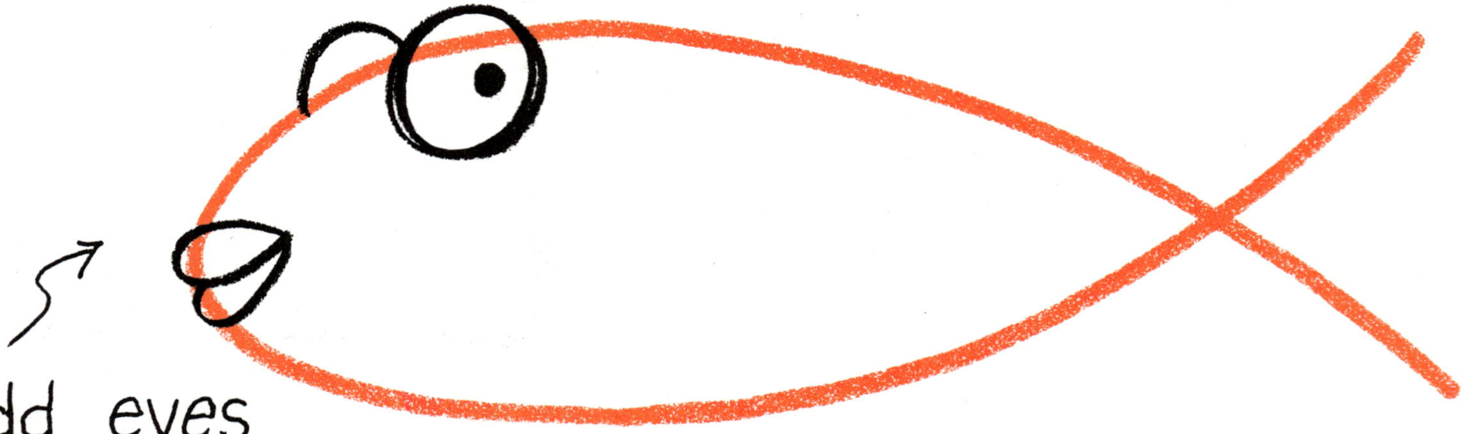

2. Add eyes and lips.

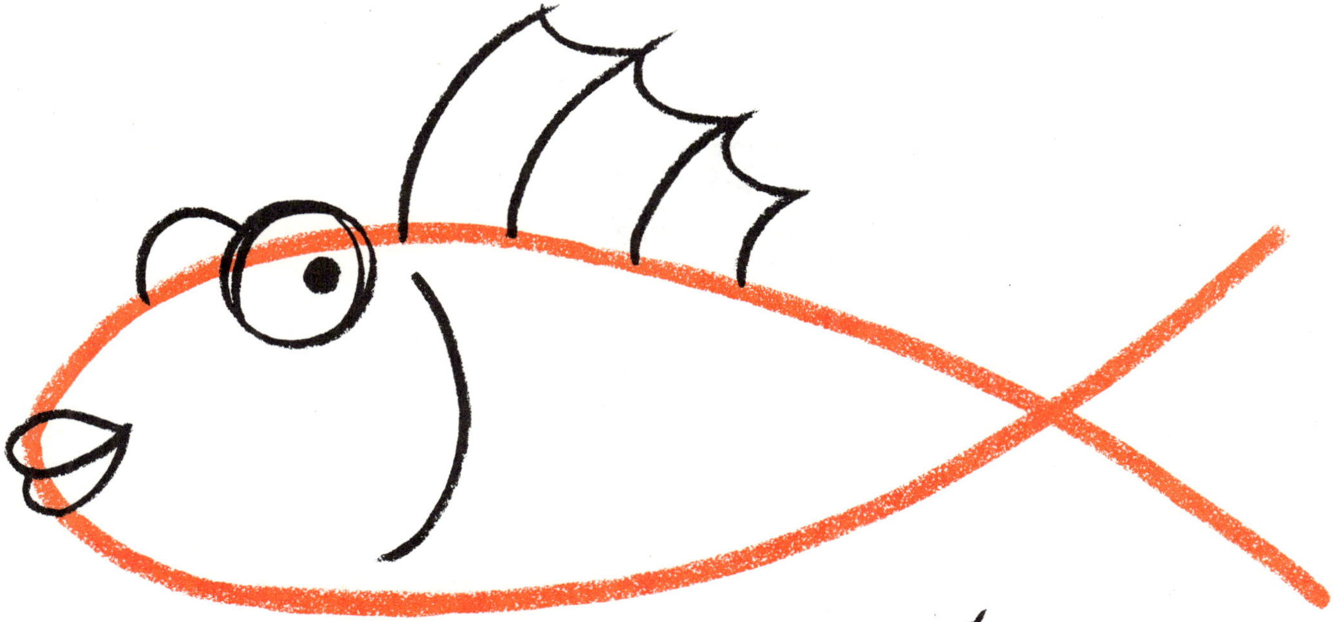

3. Draw gill and fin.

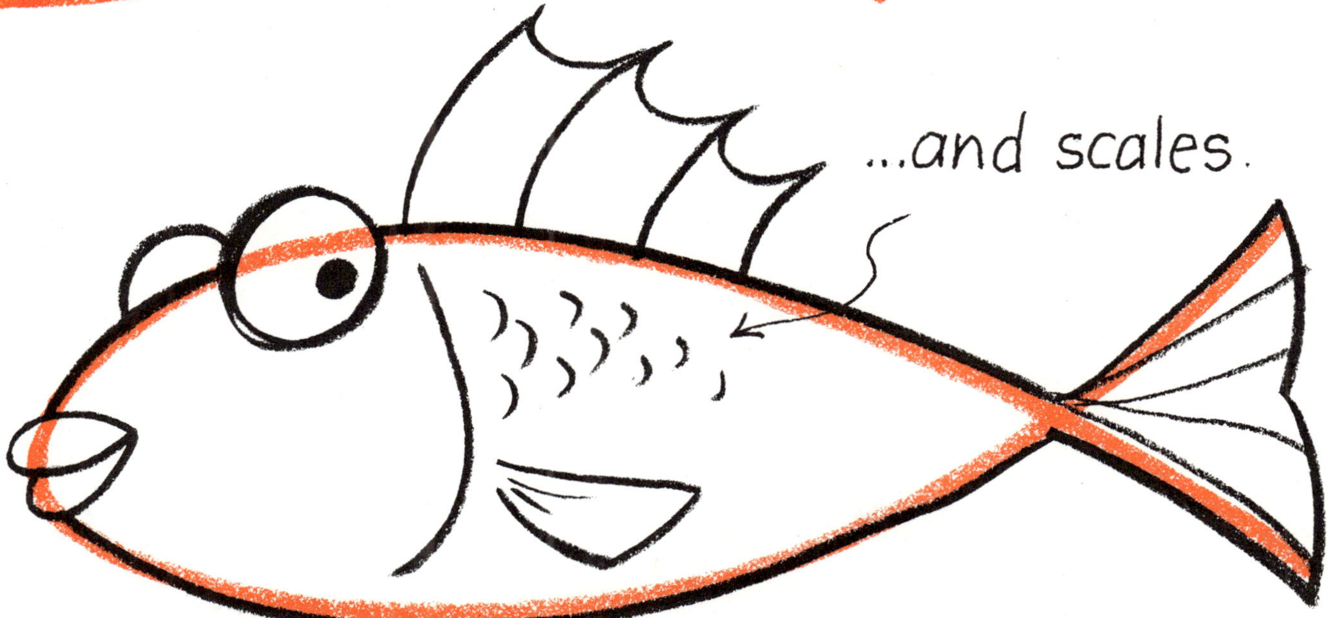

4. Add flipper and tail...

Pig

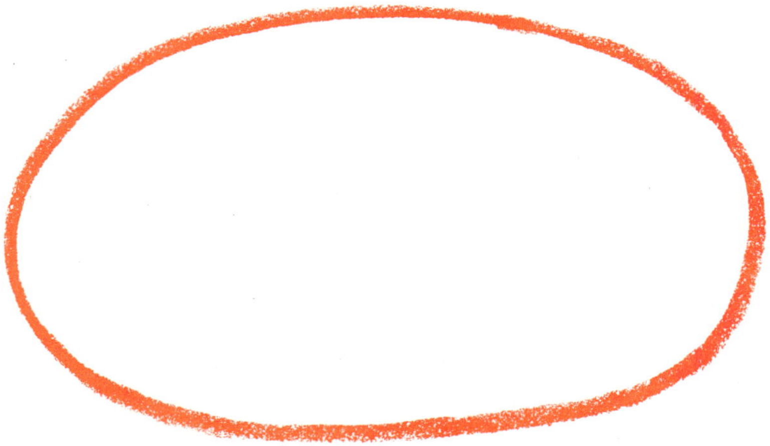

1. Draw an oval.

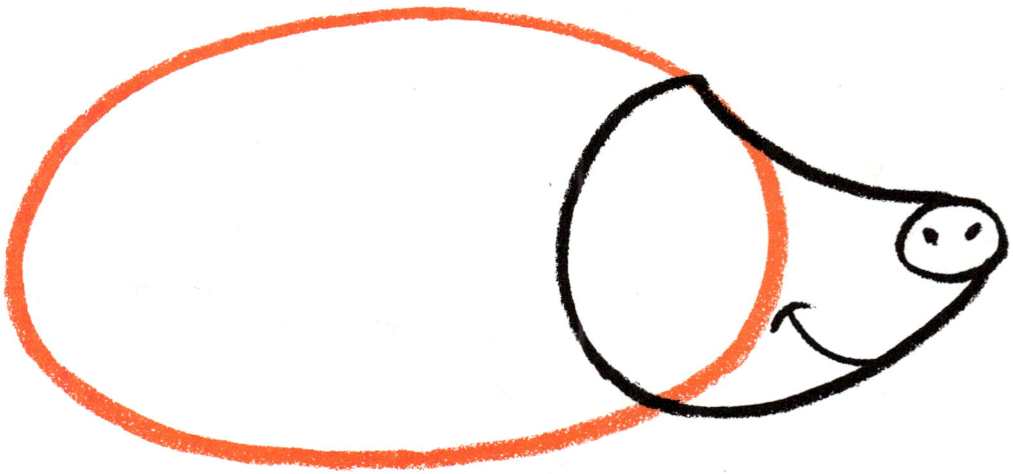

2. Add a fat head,
snout and mouth.

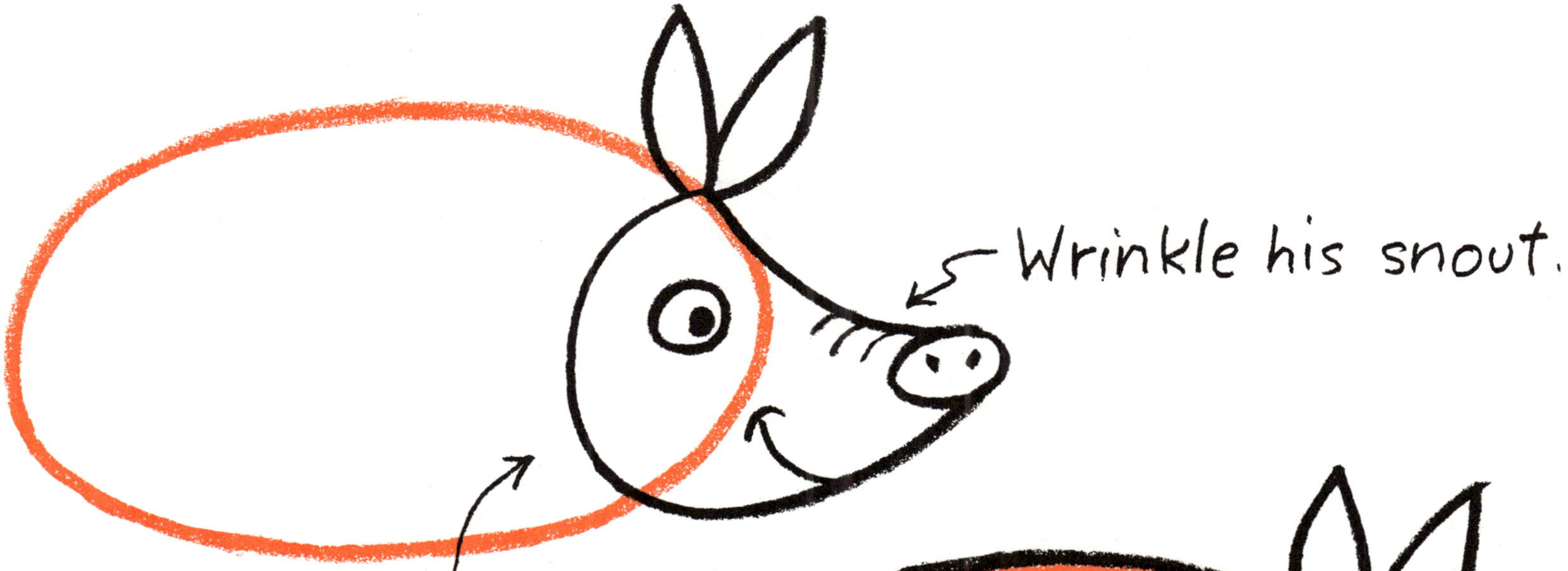

3. Add an eye and two ears.

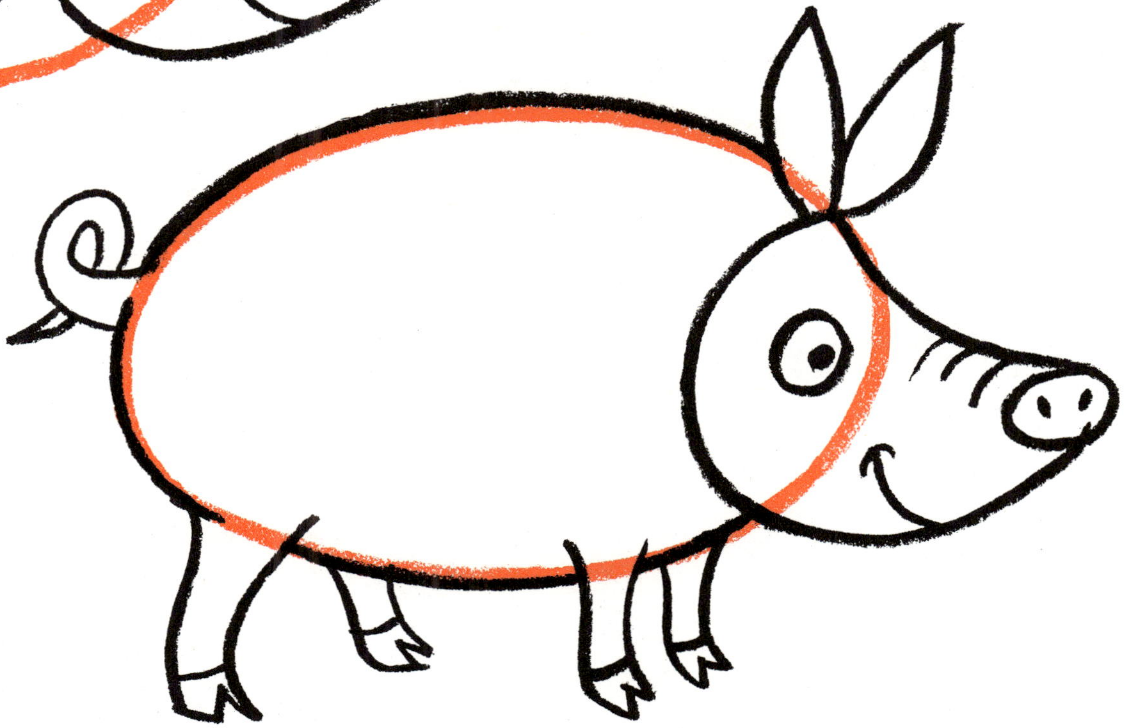

4. Draw four legs + hoofs and a curly tail.

Ostrich

1. Draw a rectangle.

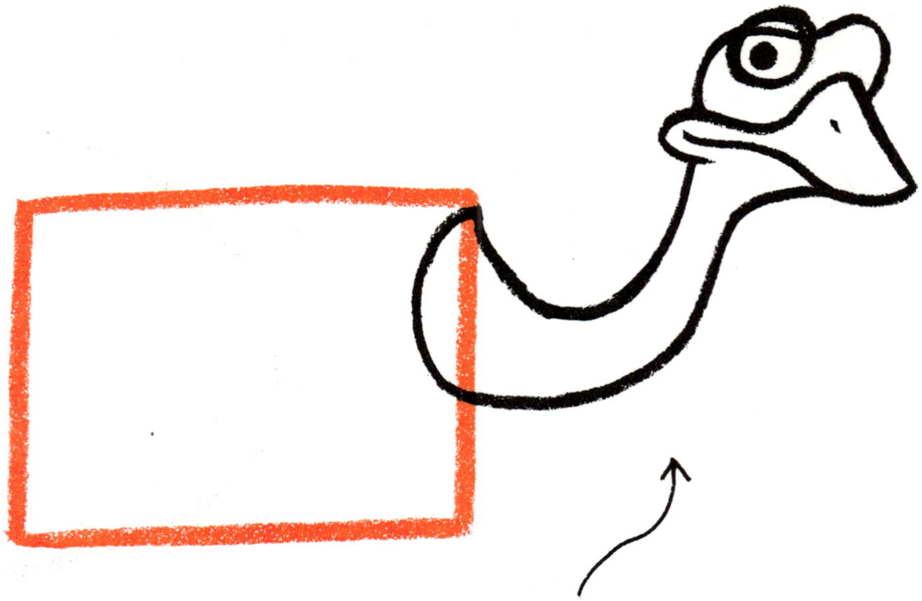

2. Add a long neck, big eye, and beak.

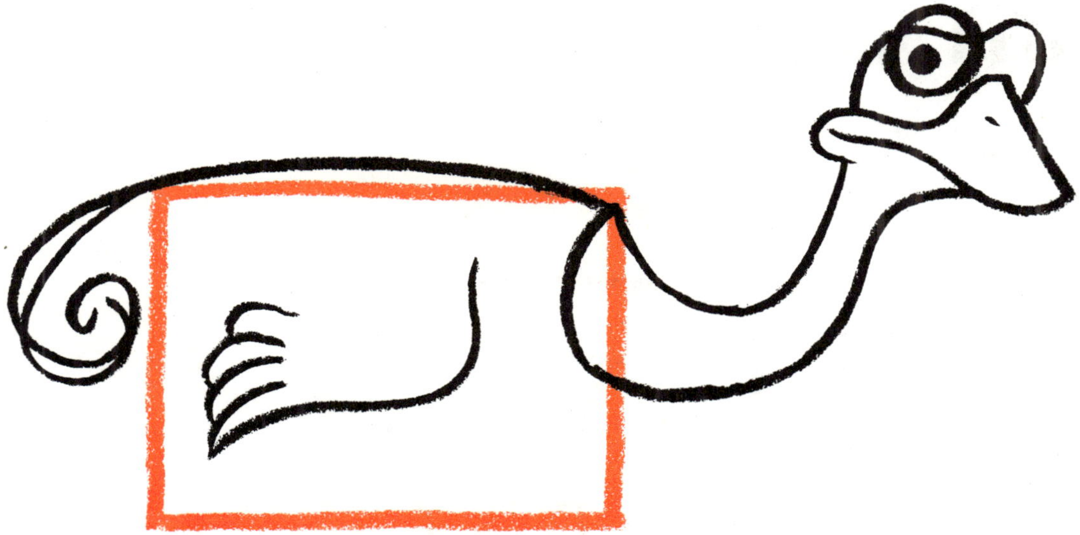

3. Draw his back ending in a fluffy tail. Add a small wing.

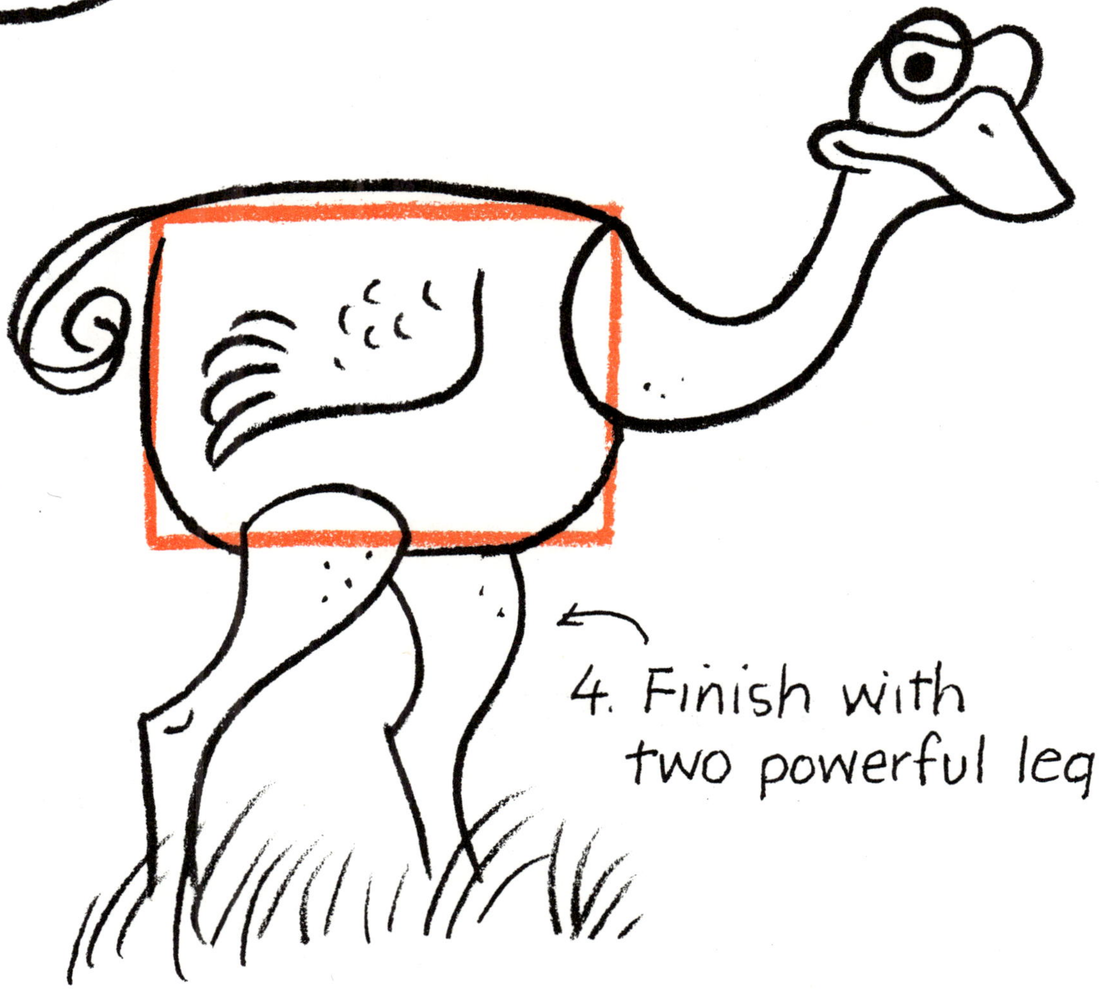

4. Finish with two powerful legs.

Barn Owl

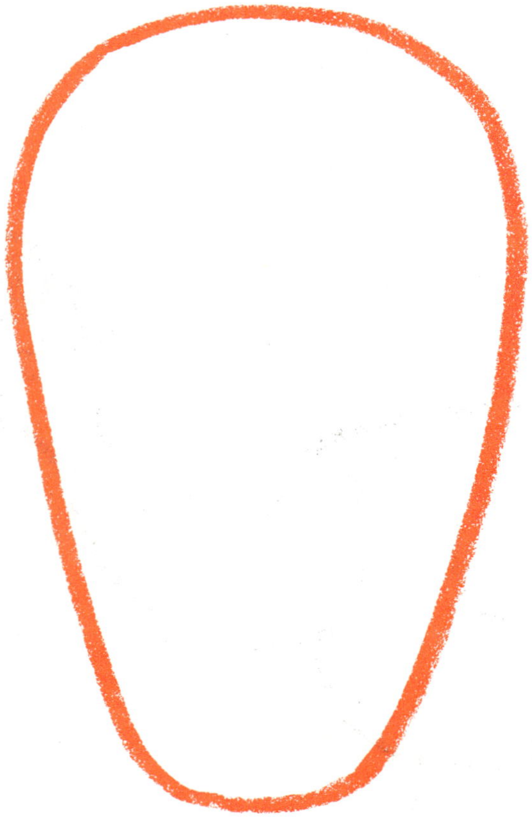

1. Draw this shape.

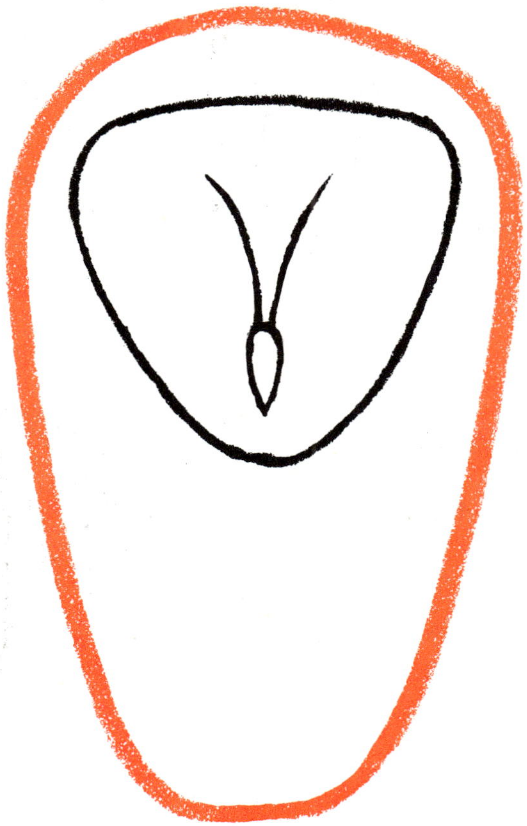

2. Add face shape and lines to beak.

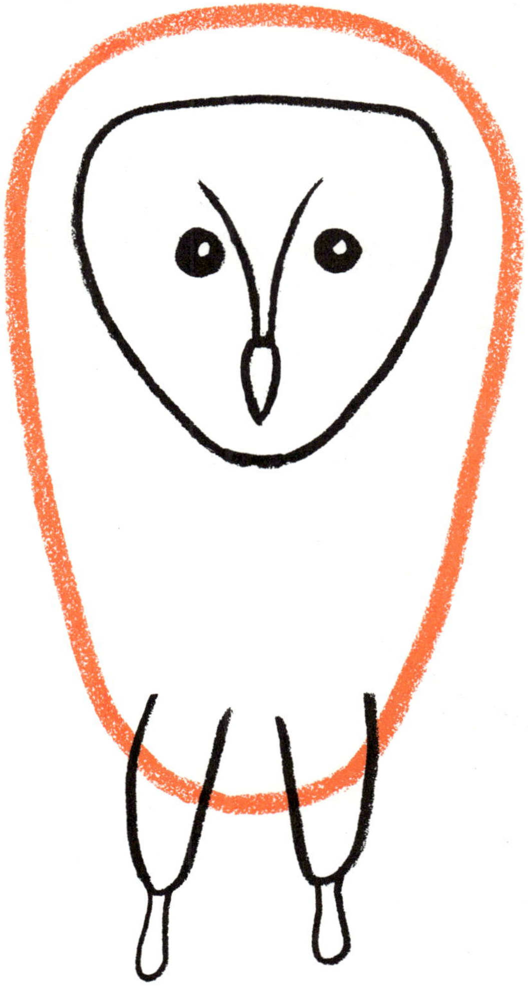

3. Draw eyes and start legs.

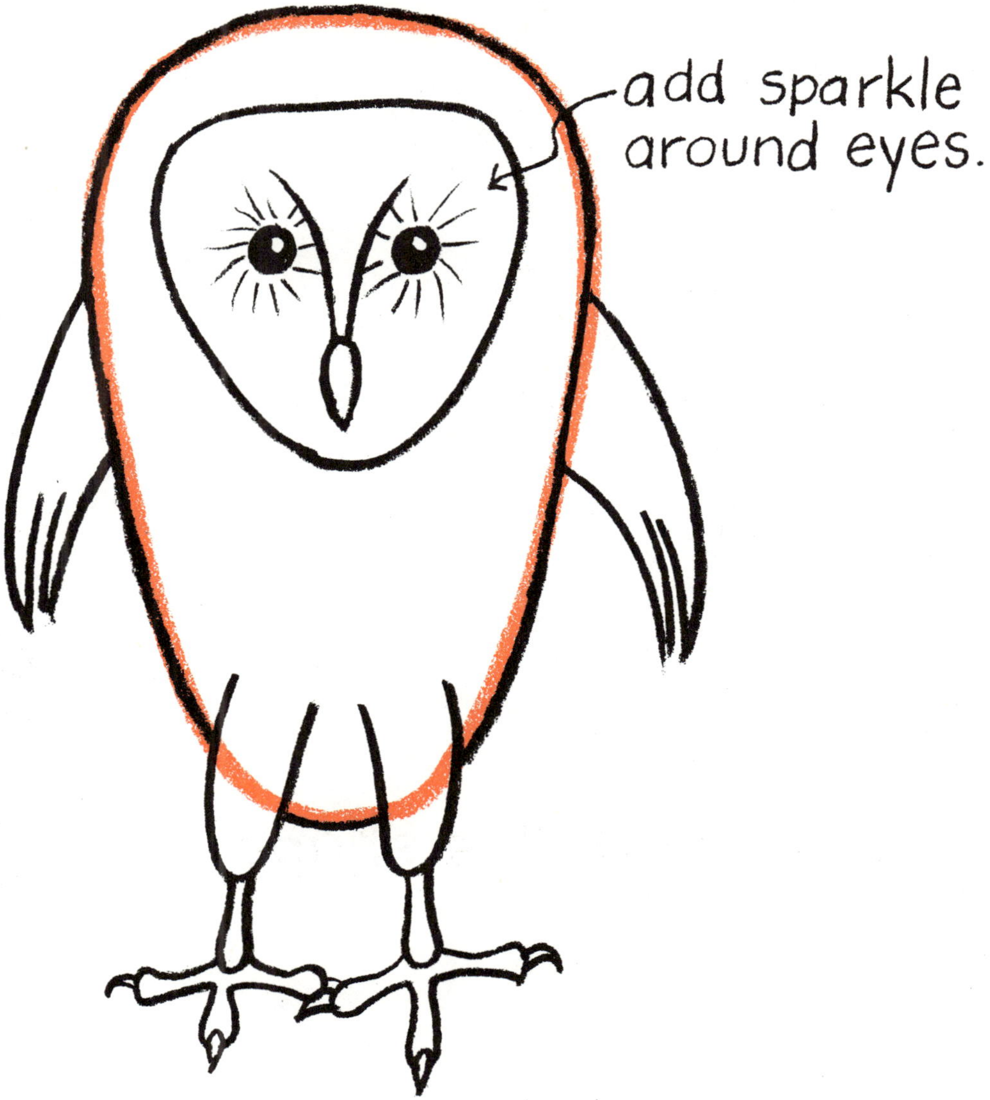

4. Finish with wings, feet and claws.

Blue Jay

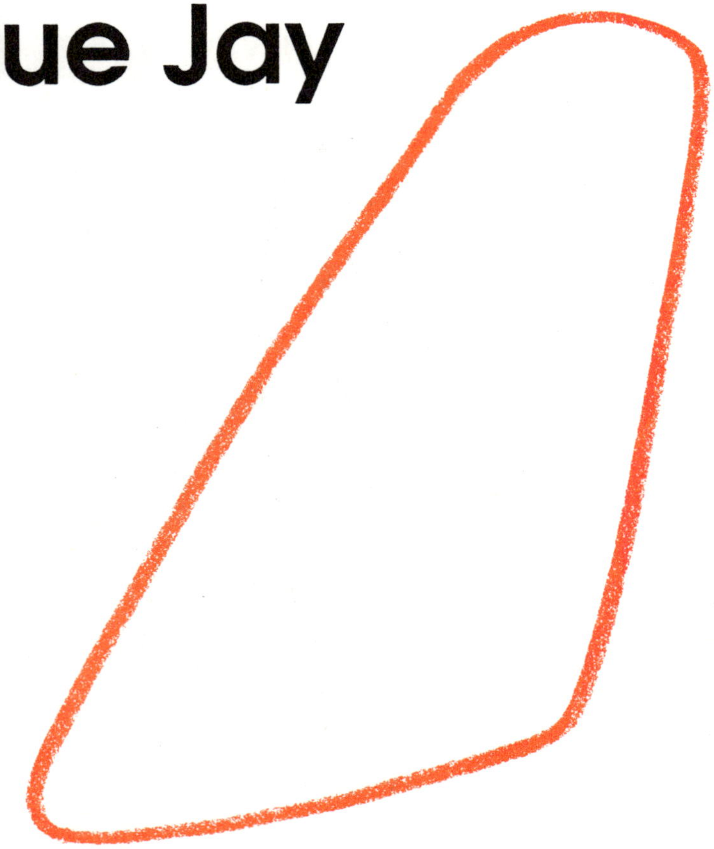

1. Start with this shape.

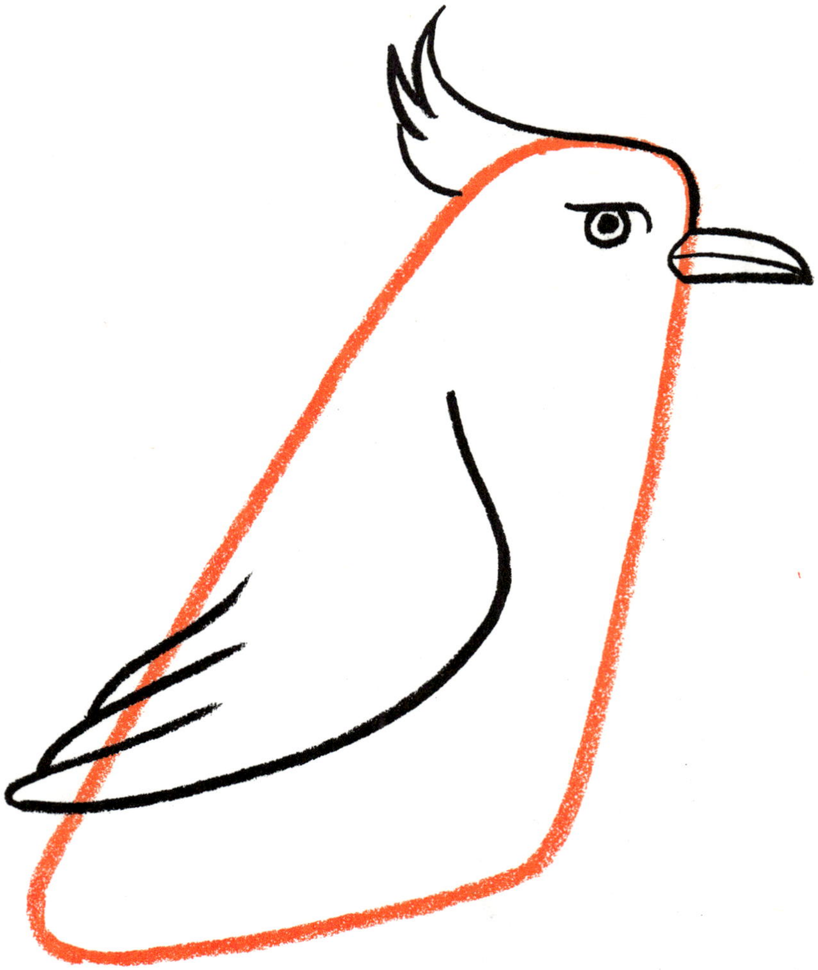

2. Add a curly tuft on his head, eye, beak and wing.

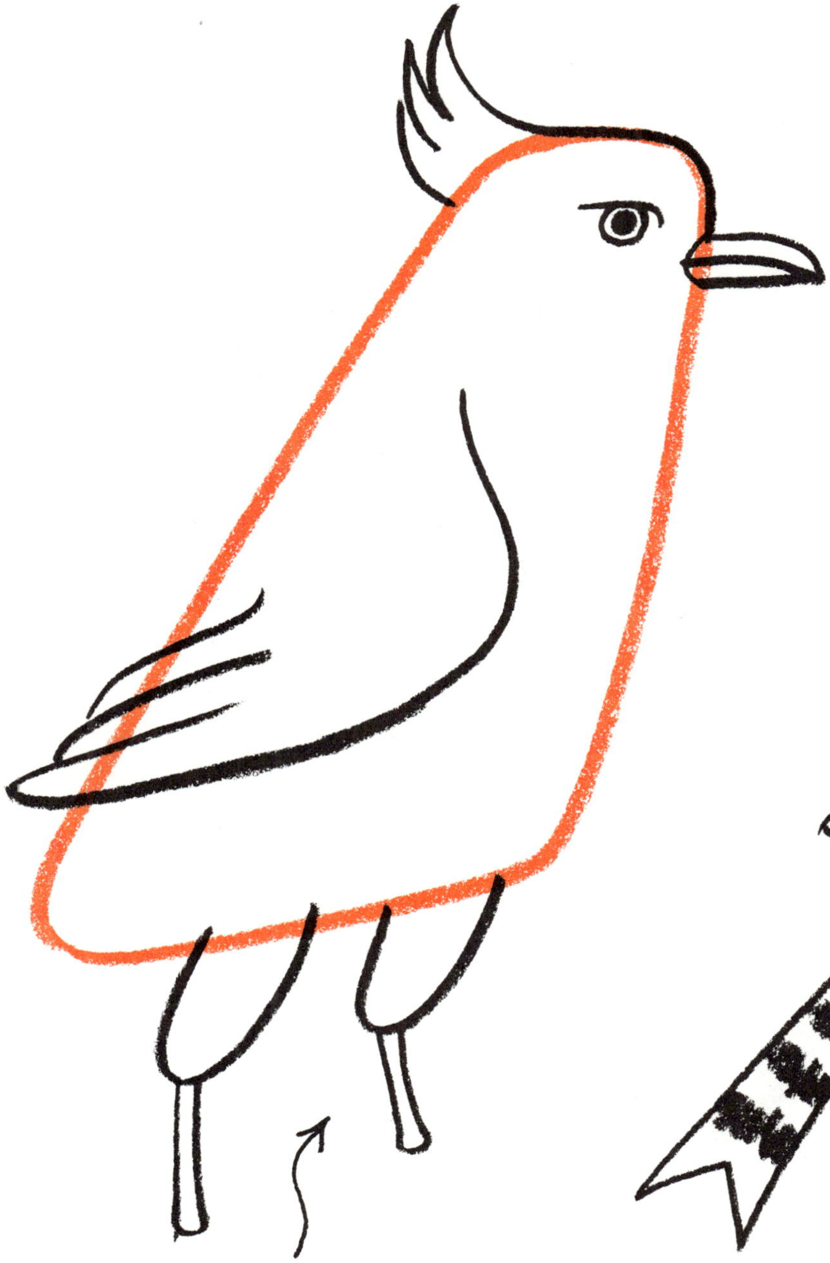

3. Draw thighs and legs.

4. Finish with toes, claws and markings.

Bear

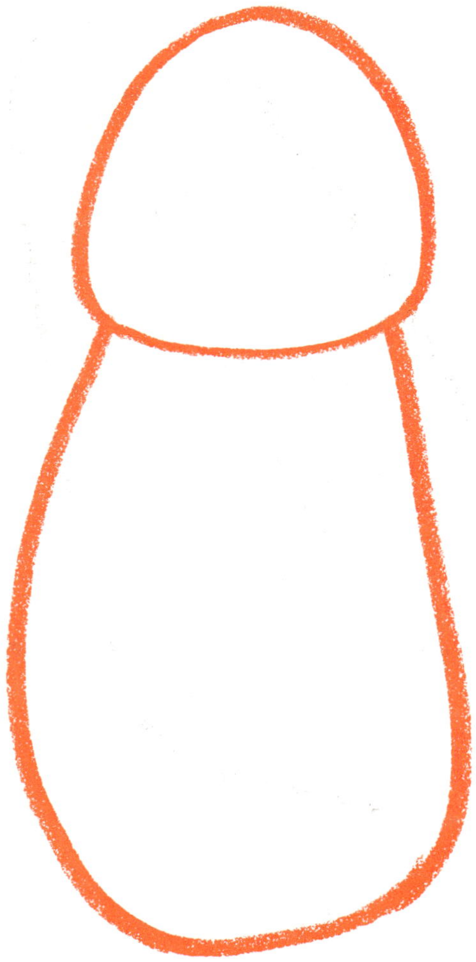

1. Draw these two shapes.

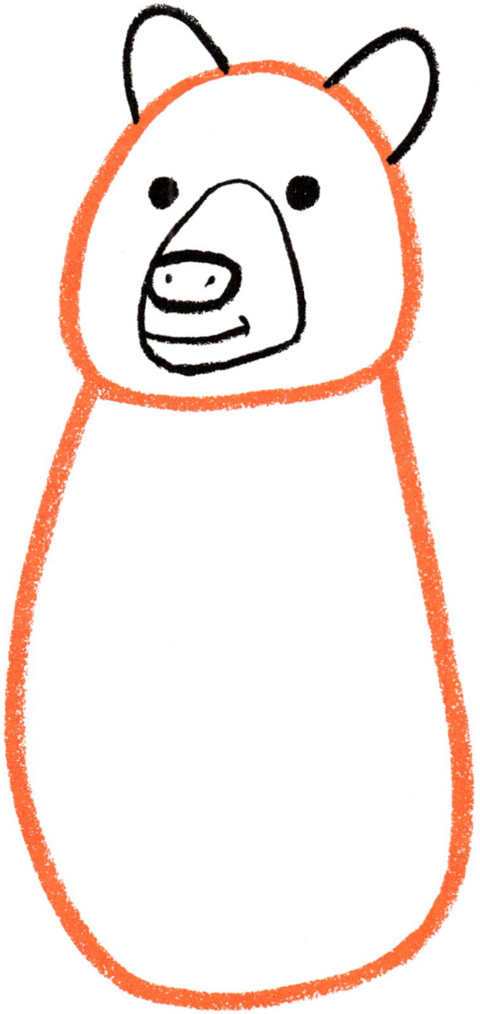

2. Add nose, mouth, eyes and ears.

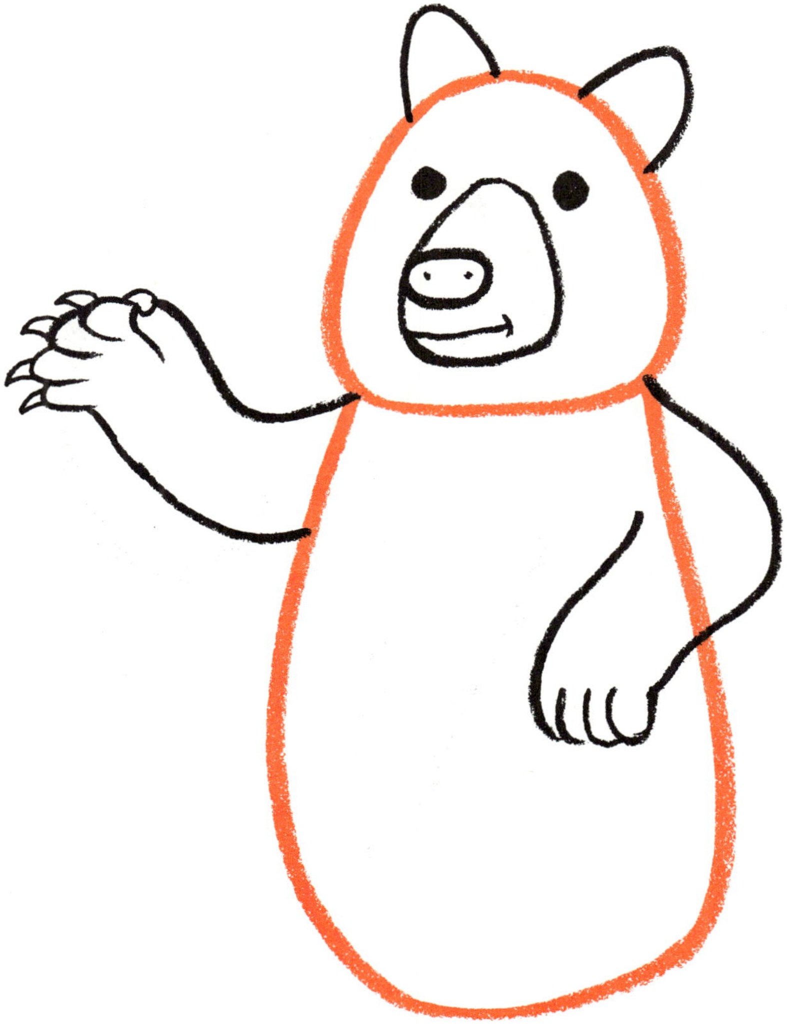

3. Draw two arms, one waving.

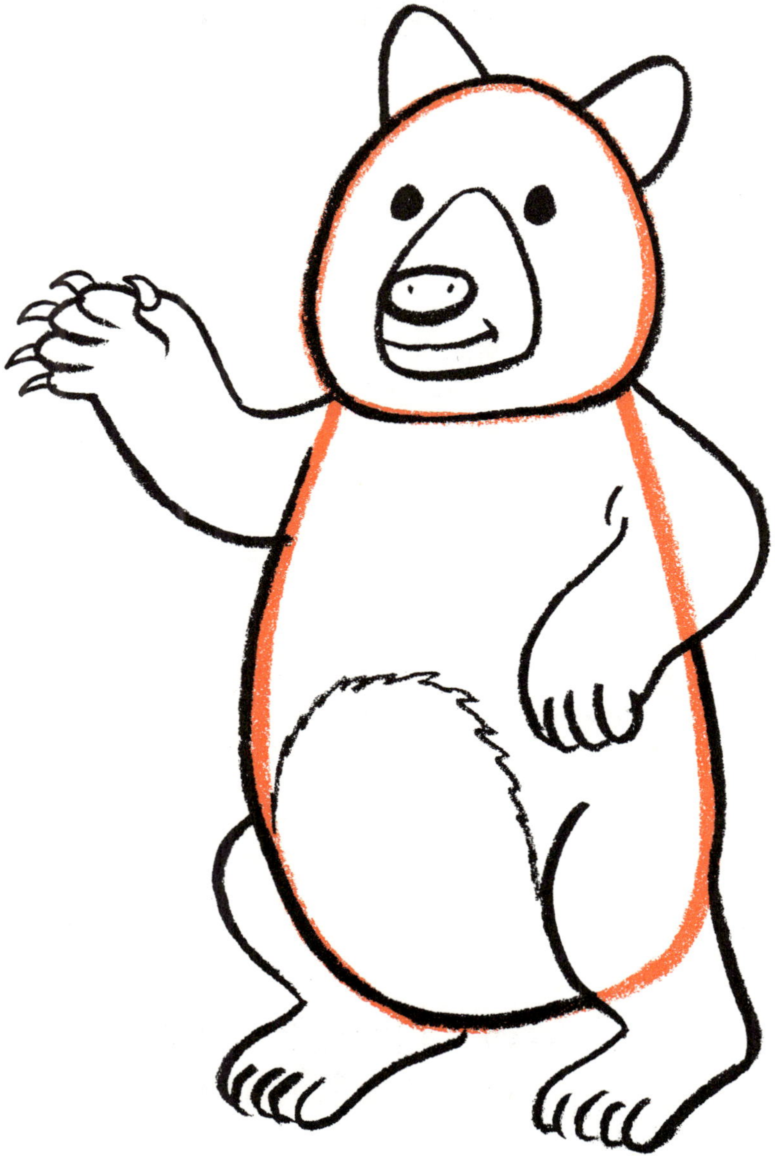

4. Finish with two feet and fuzzy pouch.

Squirrel

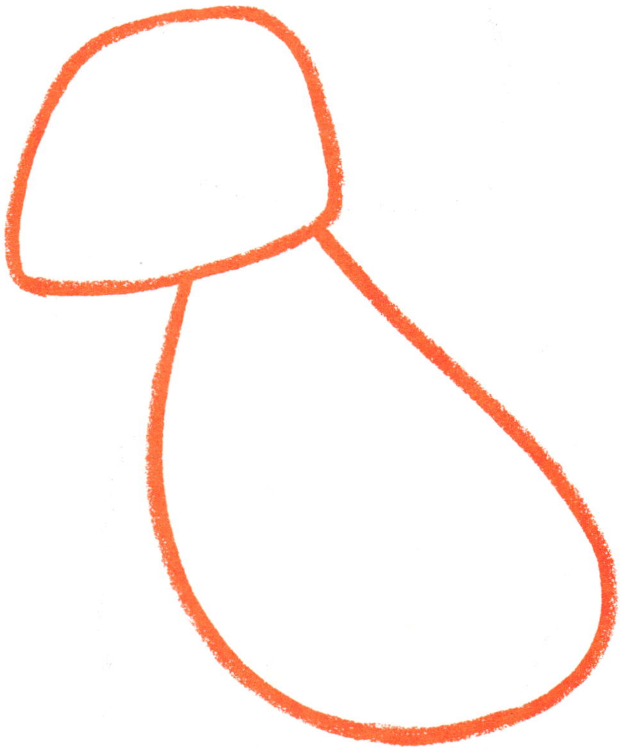

1. Draw these two shapes.

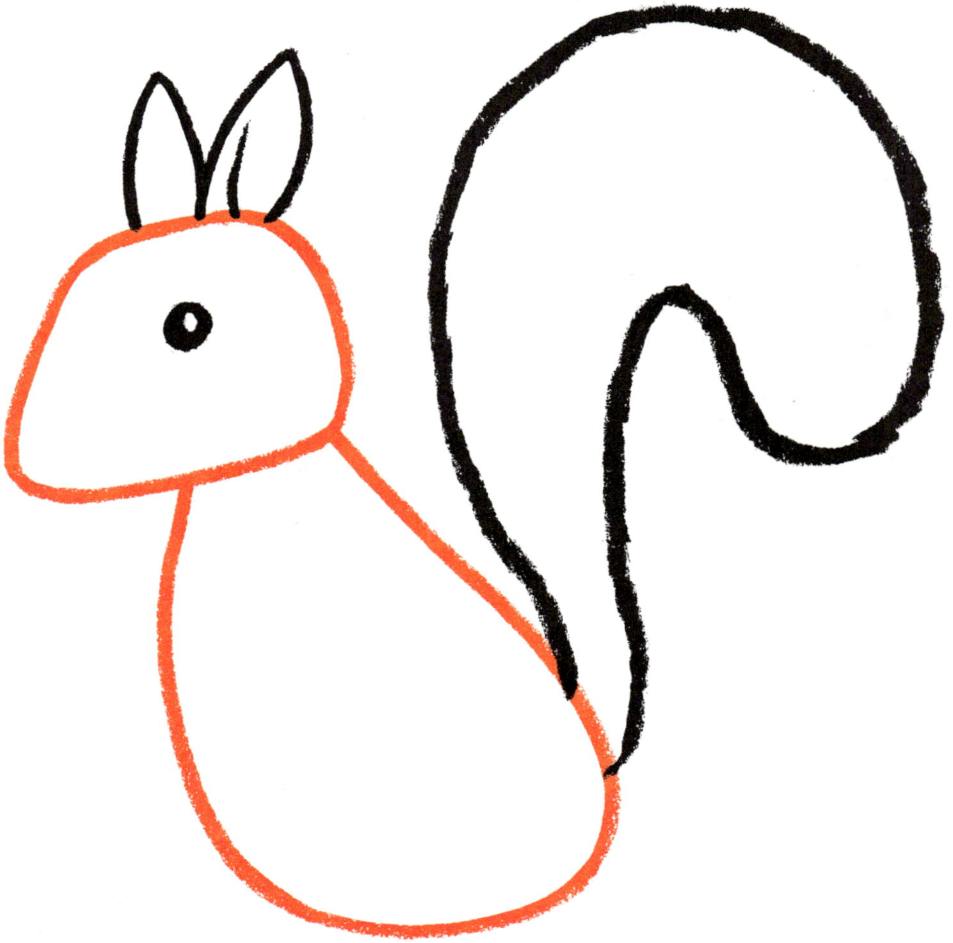

2. Add two ears, an eye, and a curved bushy tail.

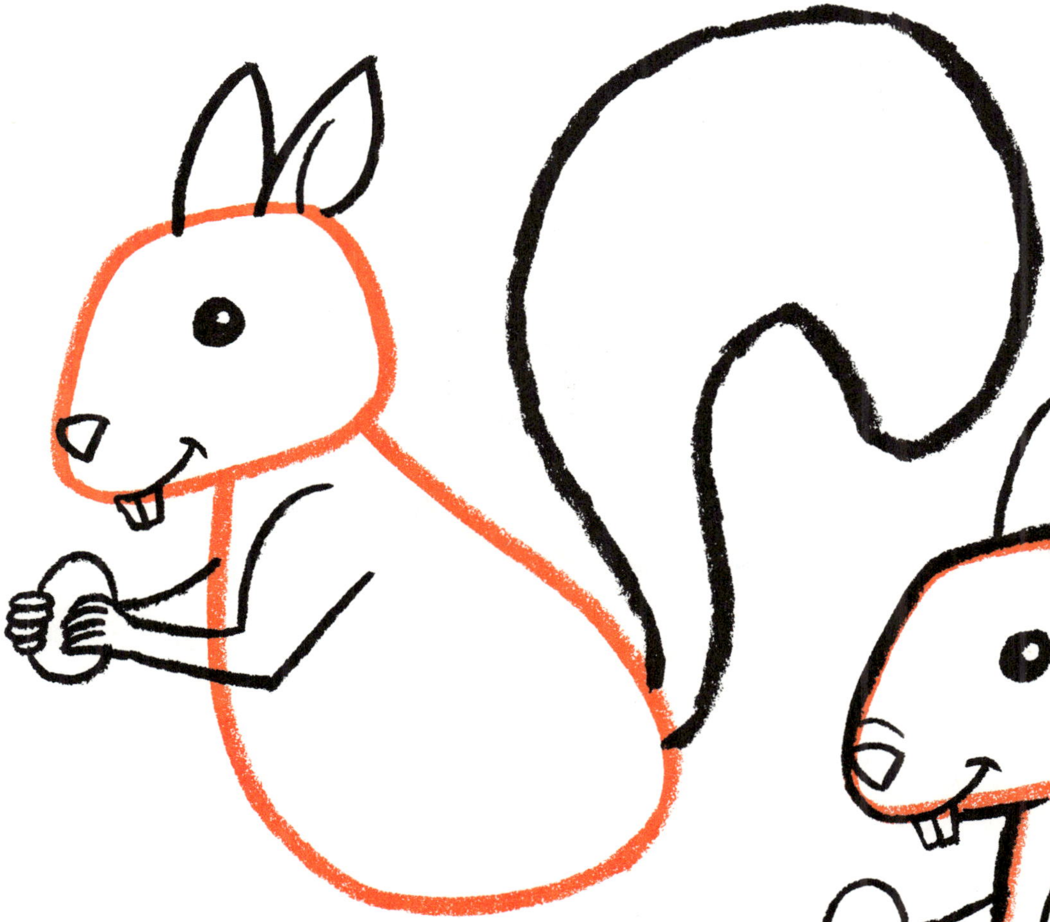

3. Draw a nose and teeth, then arms holding a nut.

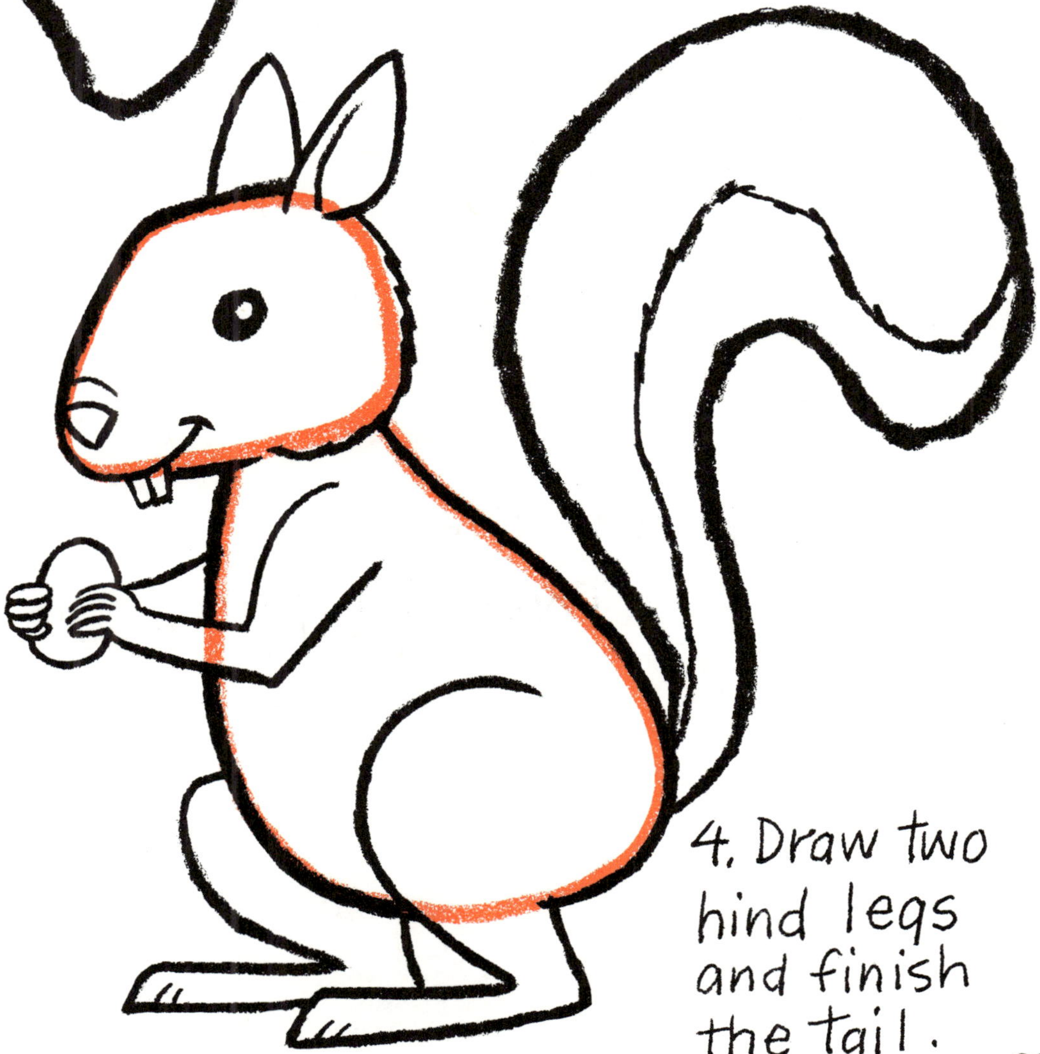

4. Draw two hind legs and finish the tail.

Frog

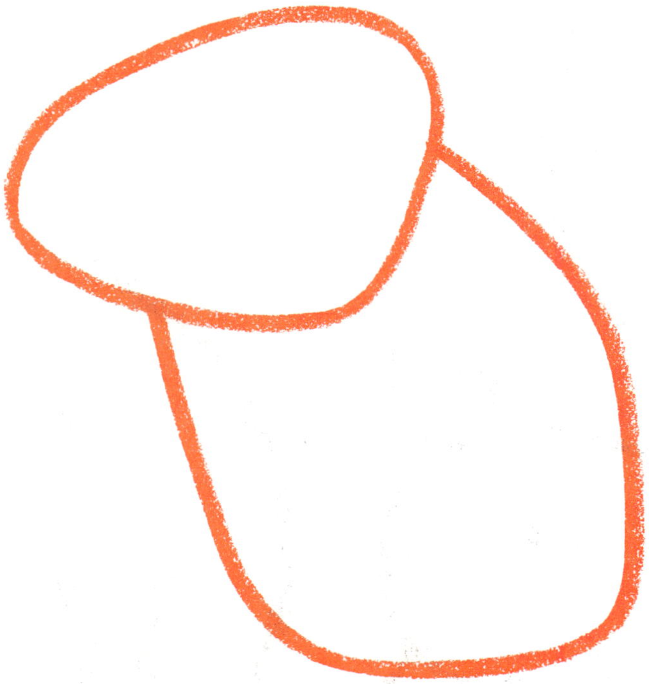

1. Draw these two shapes.

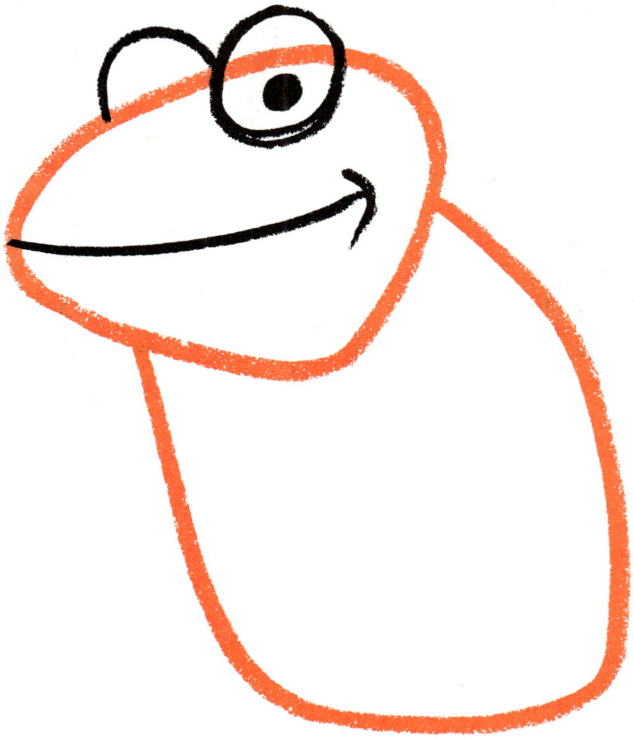

2. Add two big eyes and a long mouth.

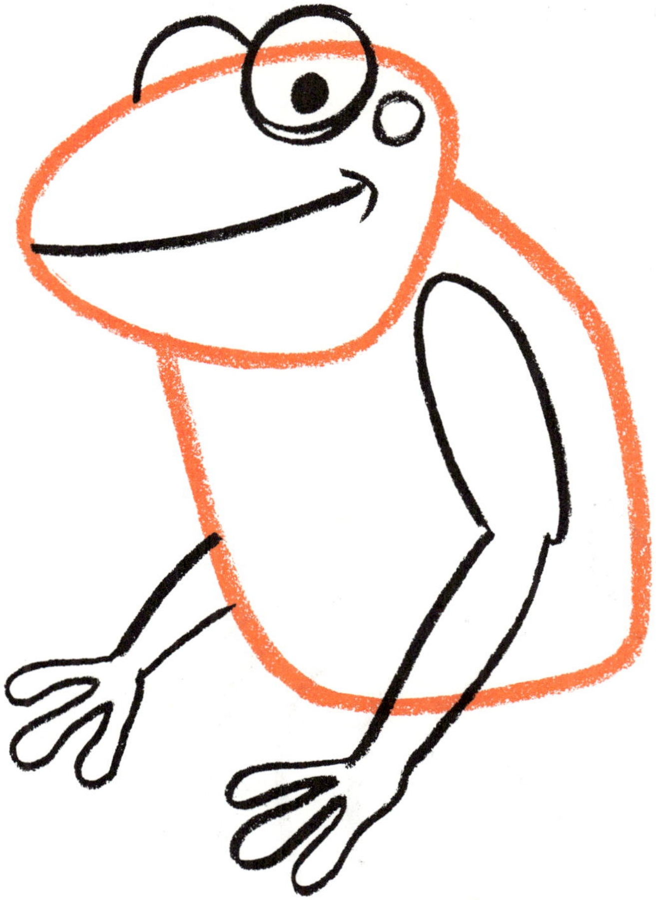

3. Now draw two front legs and fat fingers. Add a circular ear behind the eye.

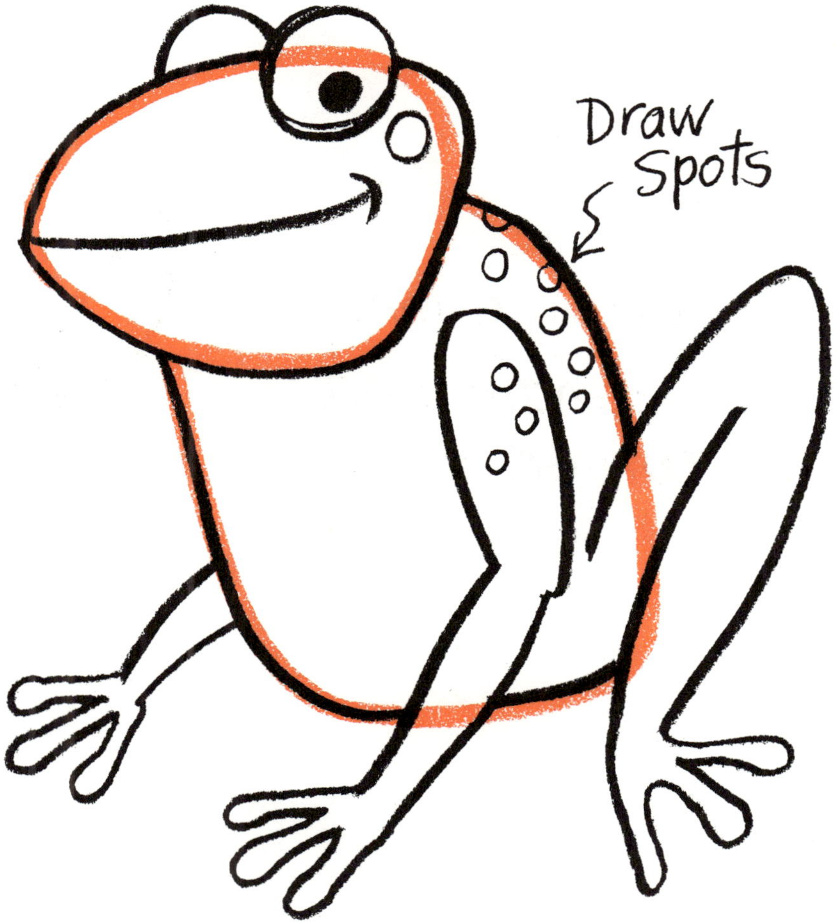

4. Add rear leg and toes.

Armadillo

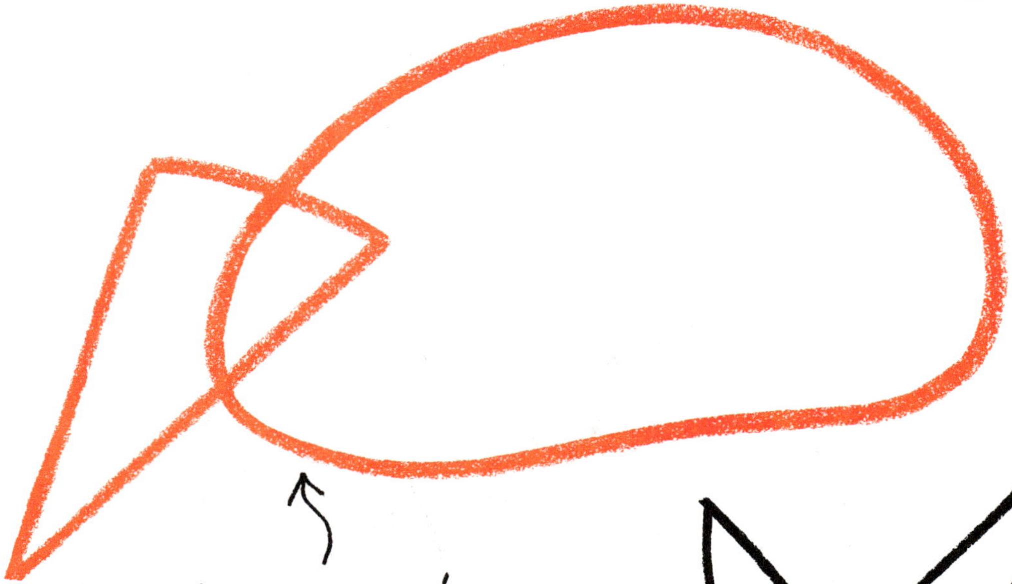

1. Draw a long triangle and curved body.

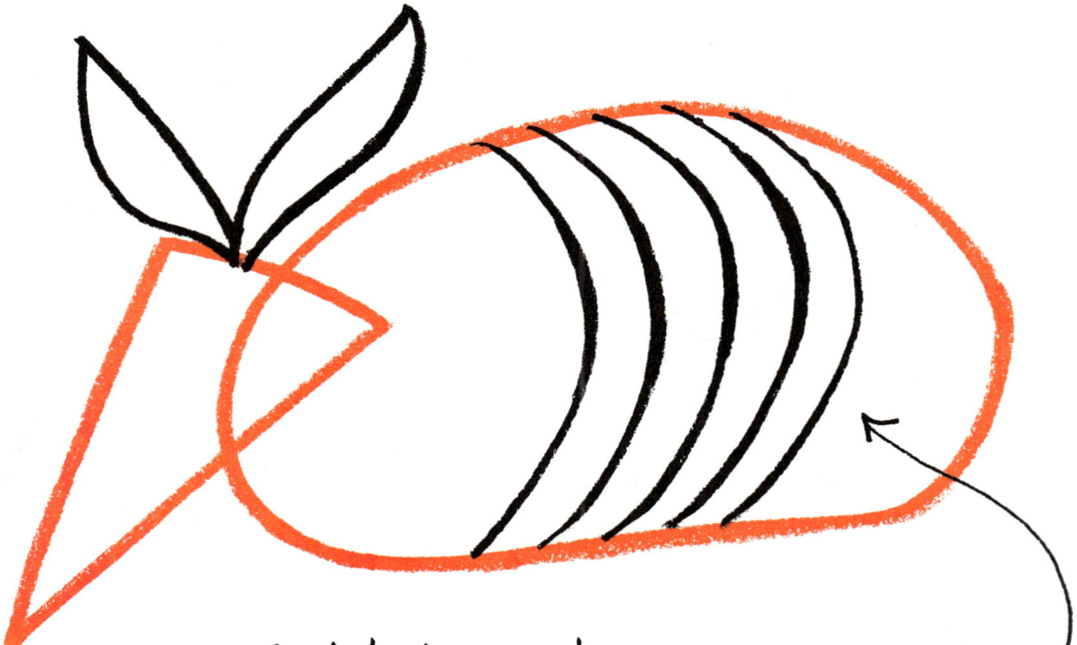

2. Add two long ears and curved rib shapes.

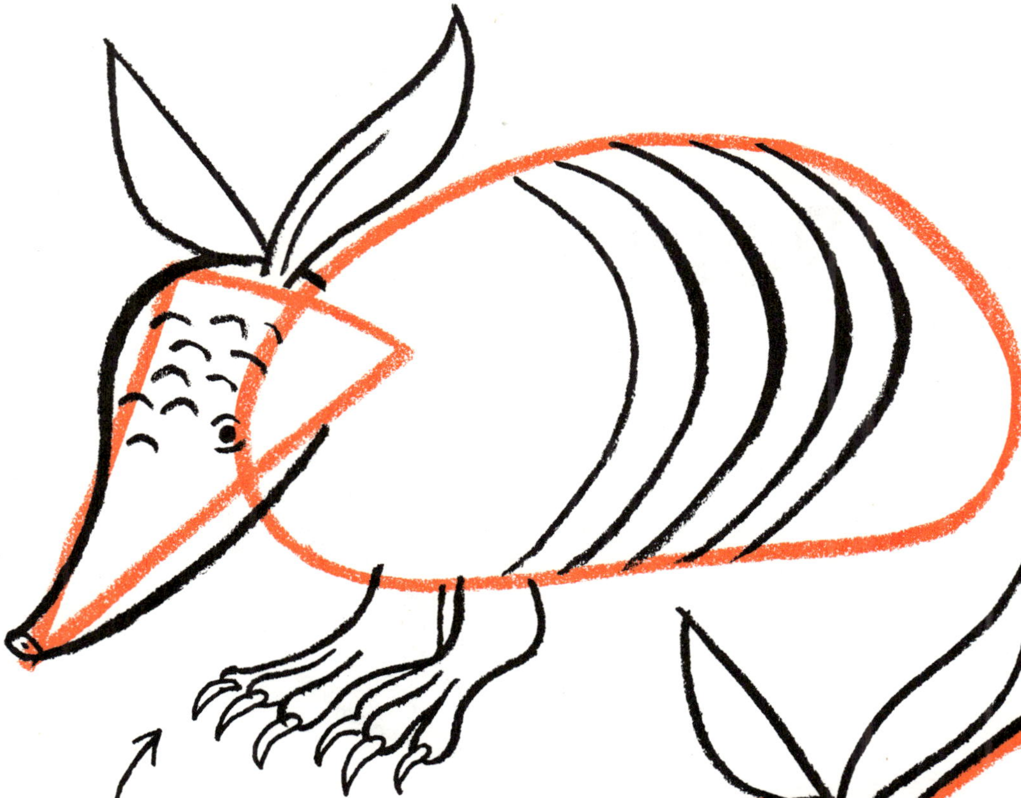

3. Draw two front legs with digging claws, and head and eye.

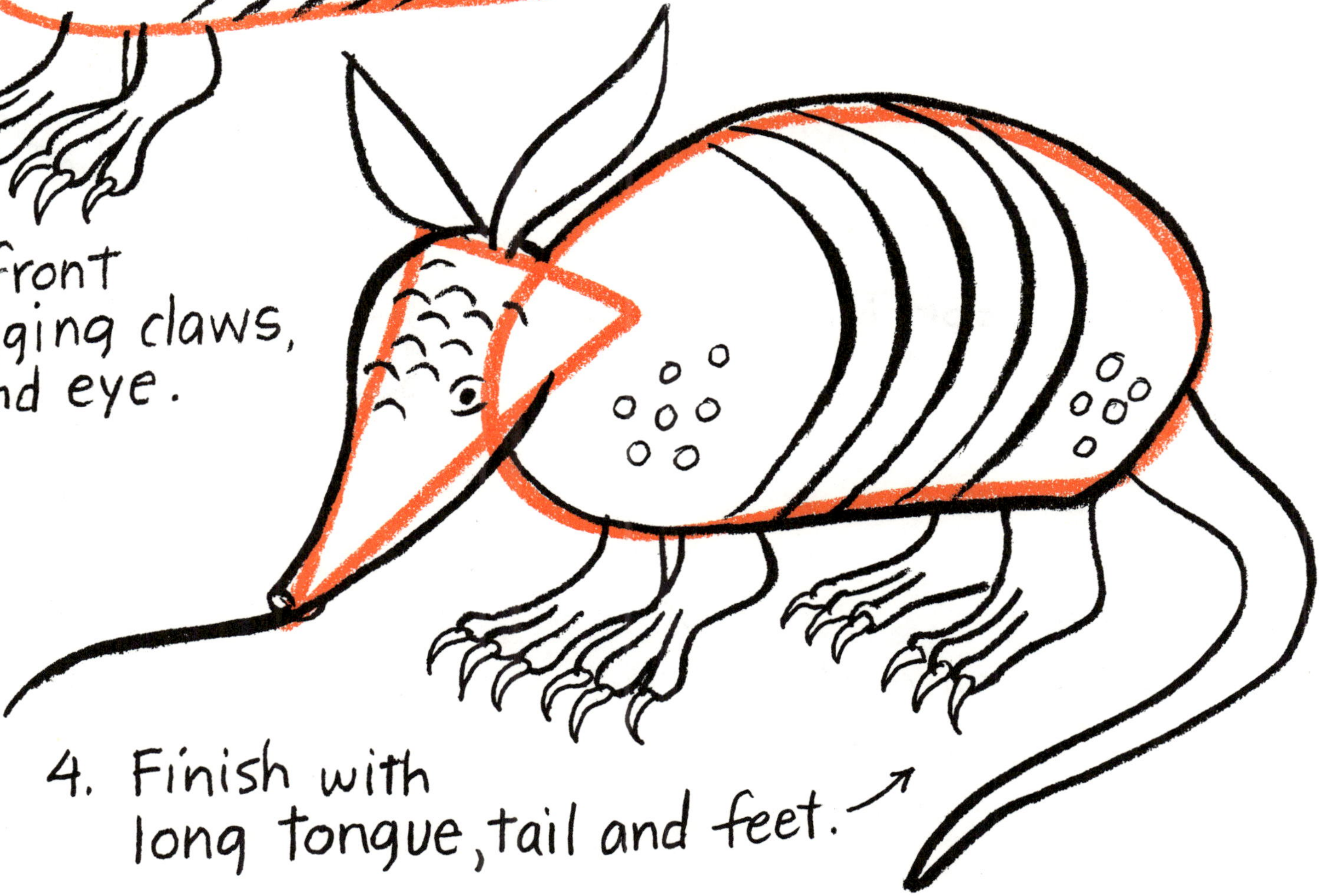

4. Finish with long tongue, tail and feet.

Rabbit

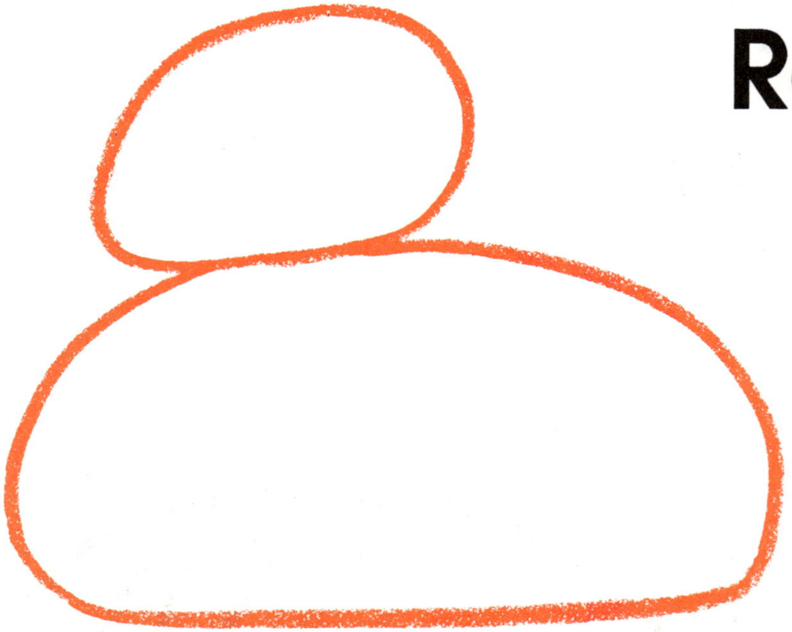

1. Draw these two shapes.

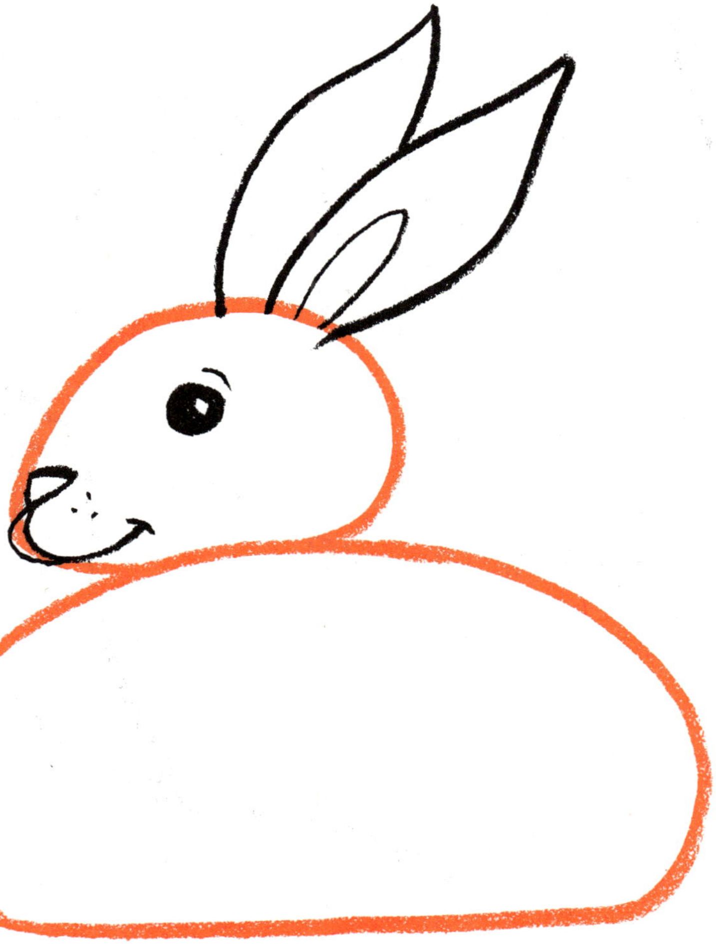

2. Start face and
two long ears.

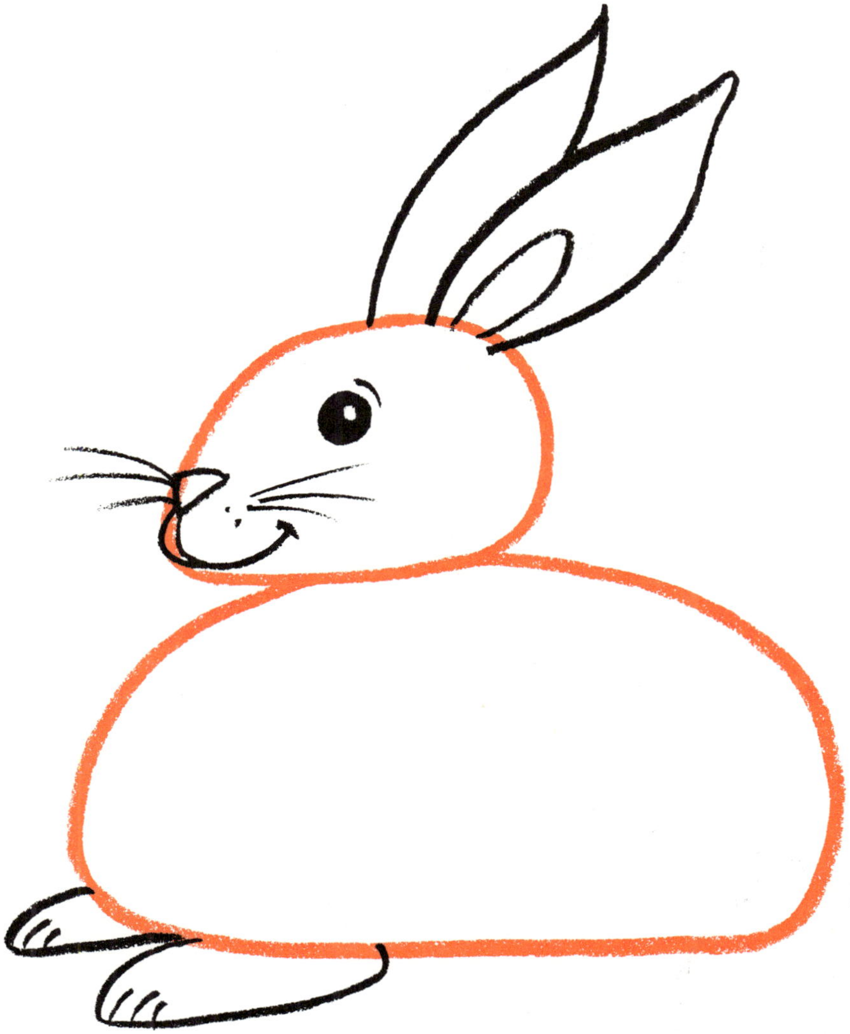

3. Add whiskers and two front paws.

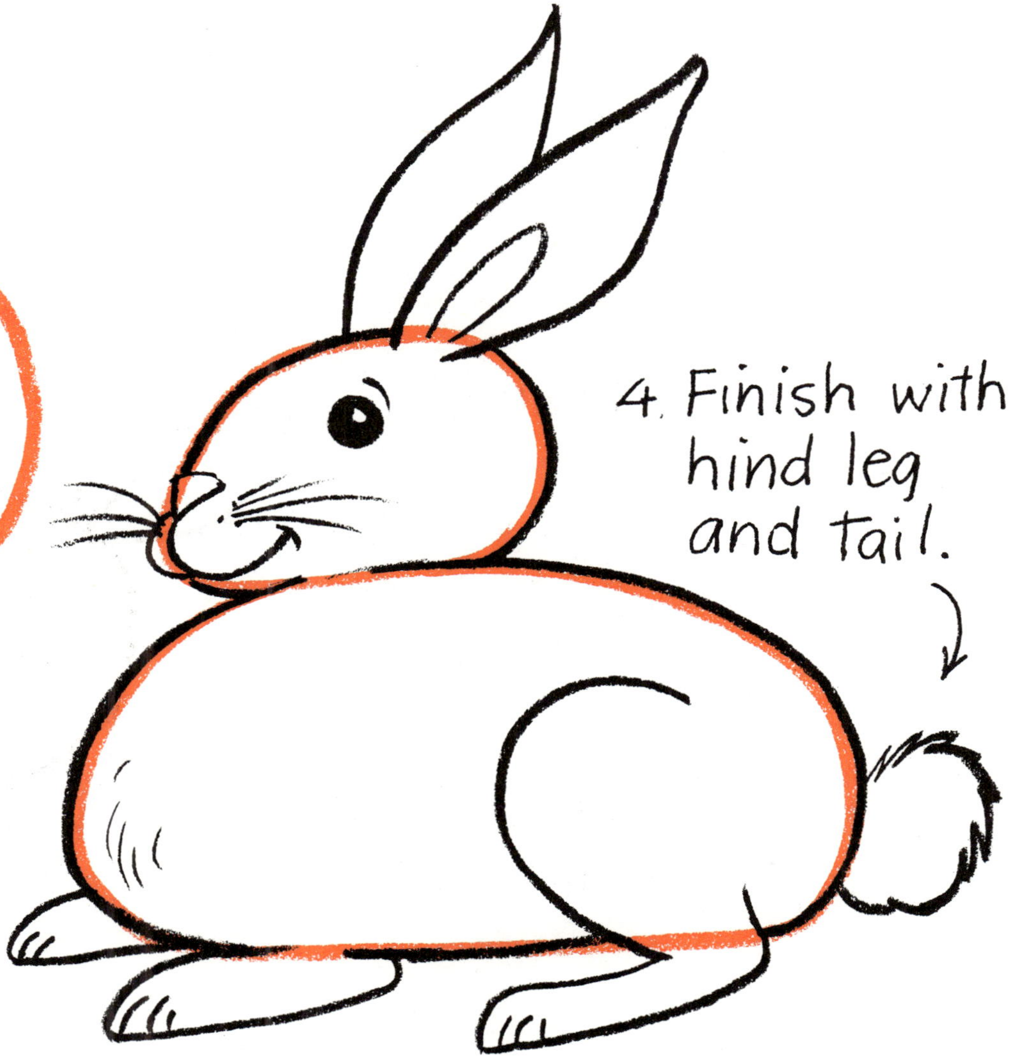

4. Finish with hind leg and tail.

Deer

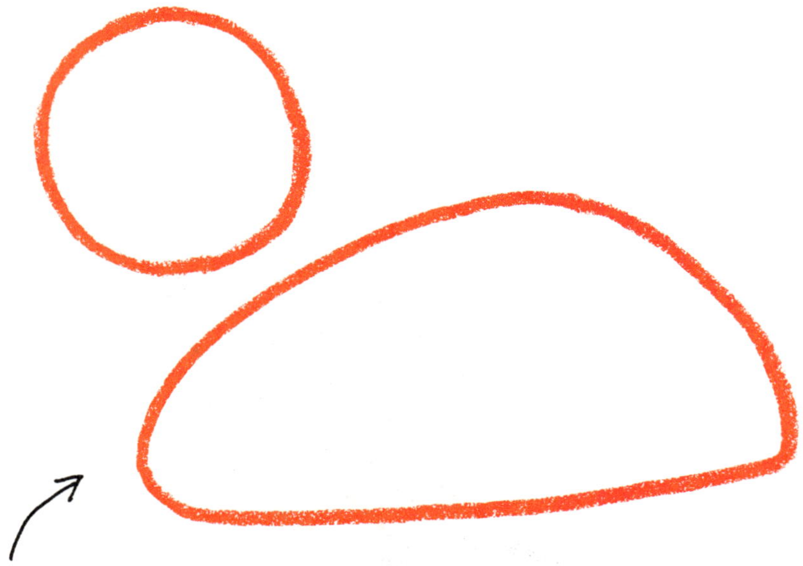

1. Draw a circle and body shape.

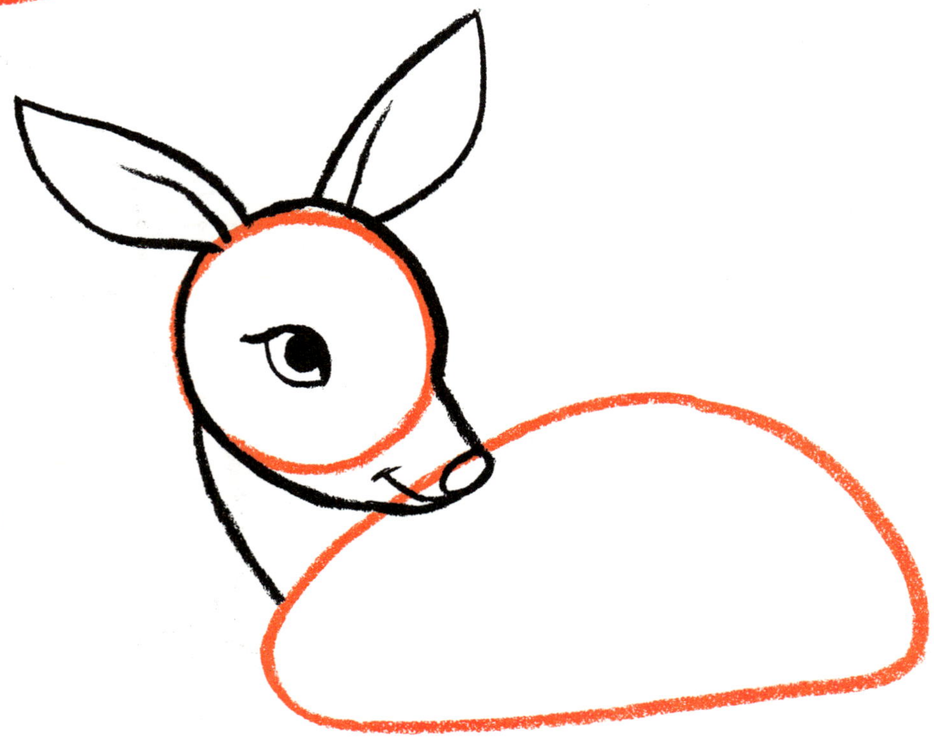

2. Draw the head with large eye and ears.

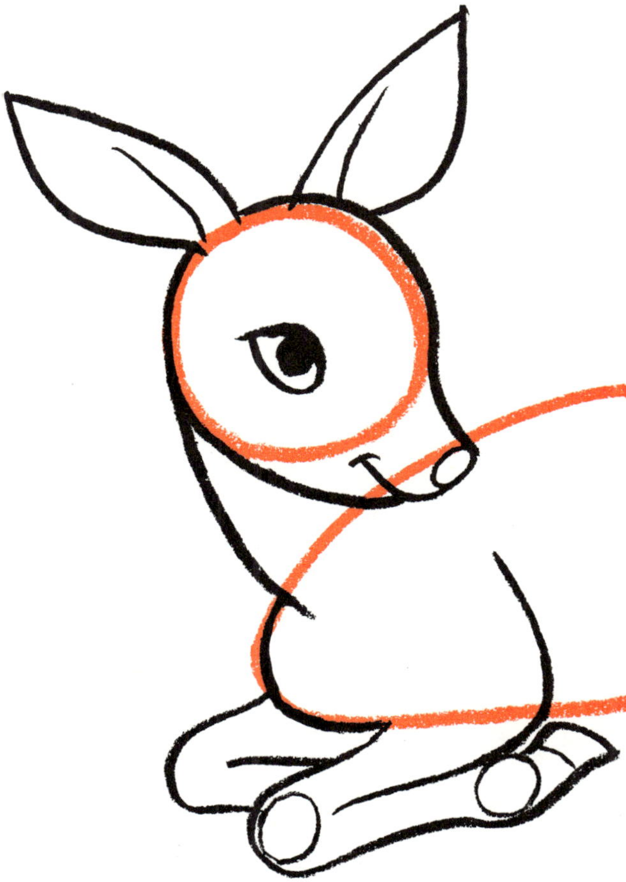

3. Add two folded legs with joints and hoofs.

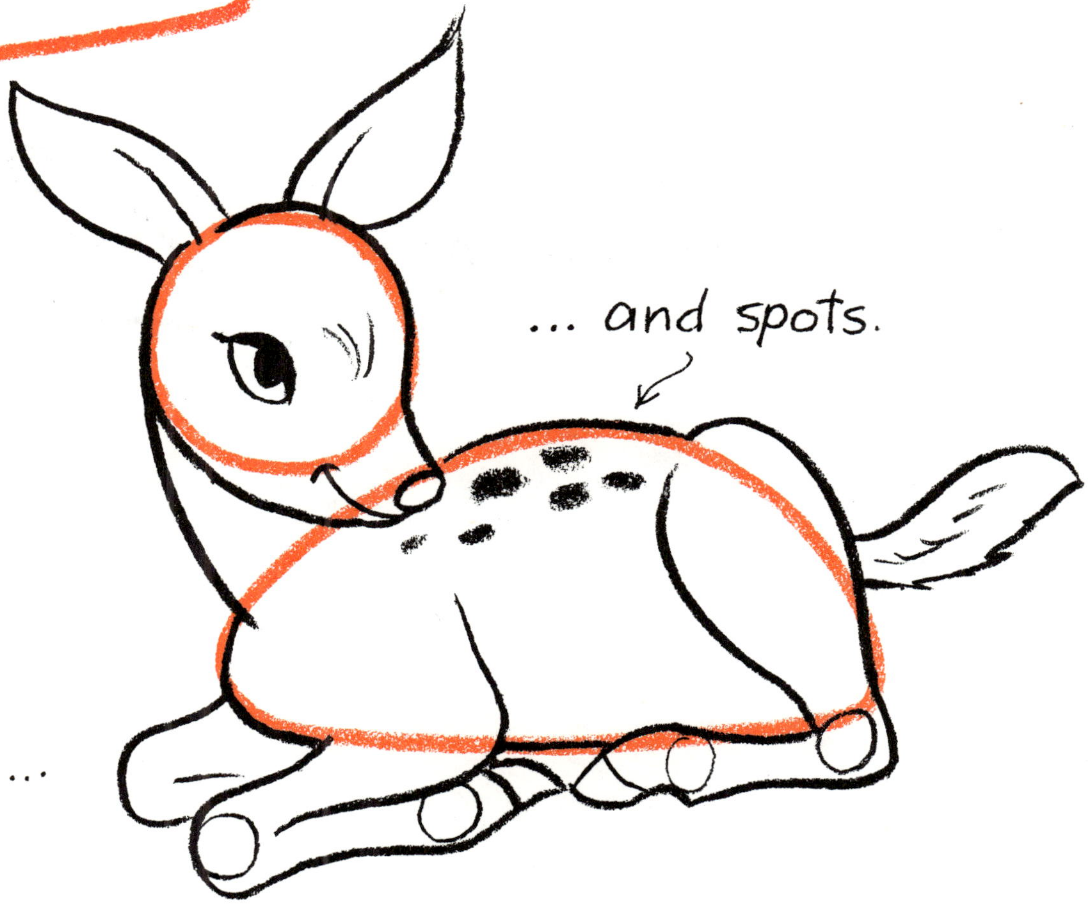

4. Finish rear leg and tail. Add a few hairs ...

... and spots.

Duck

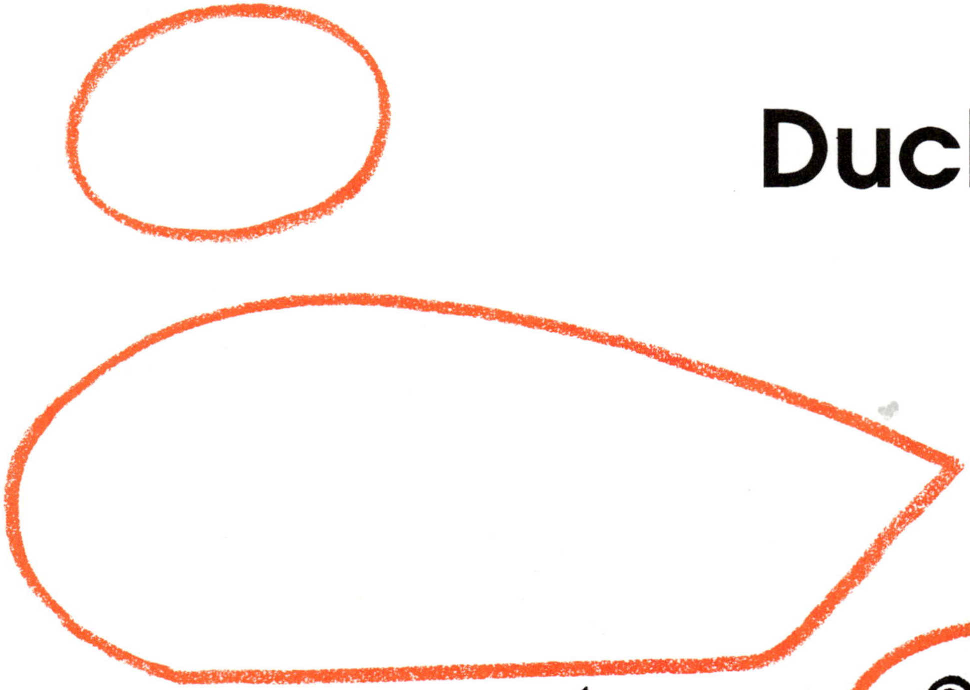

1. Start with these shapes.

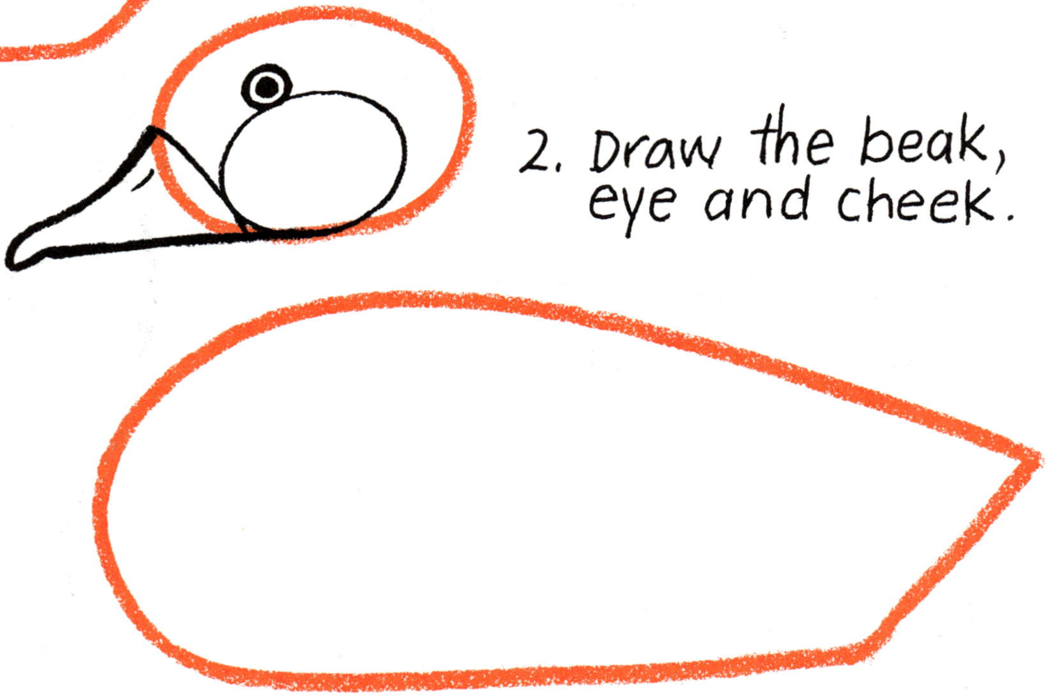

2. Draw the beak, eye and cheek.

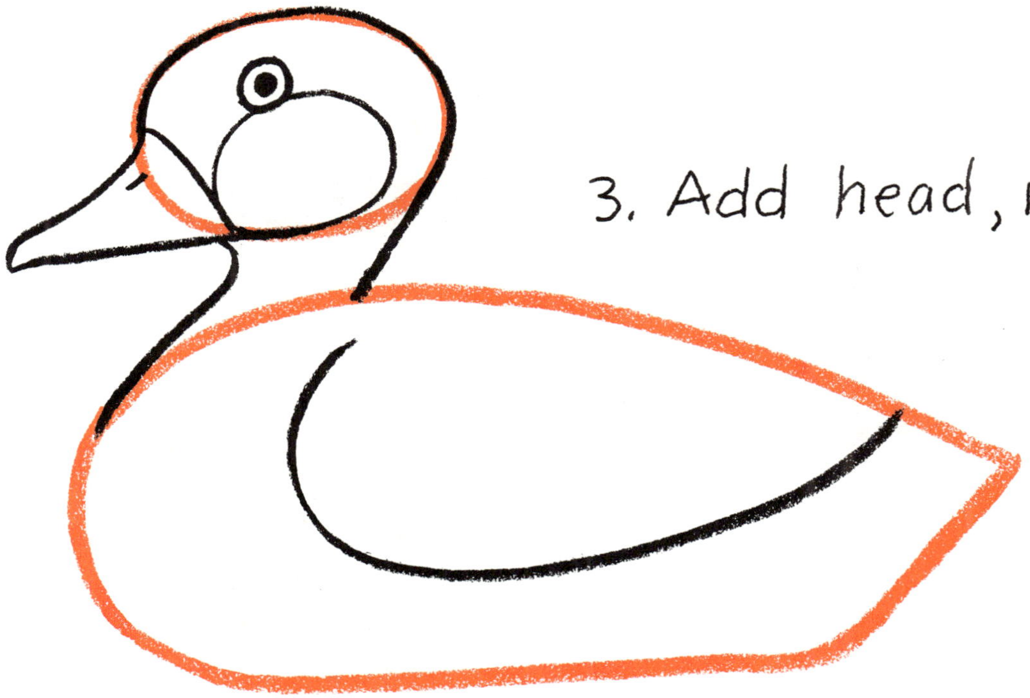

3. Add head, neck and wing.

4. Finish as shown with spots and markings.

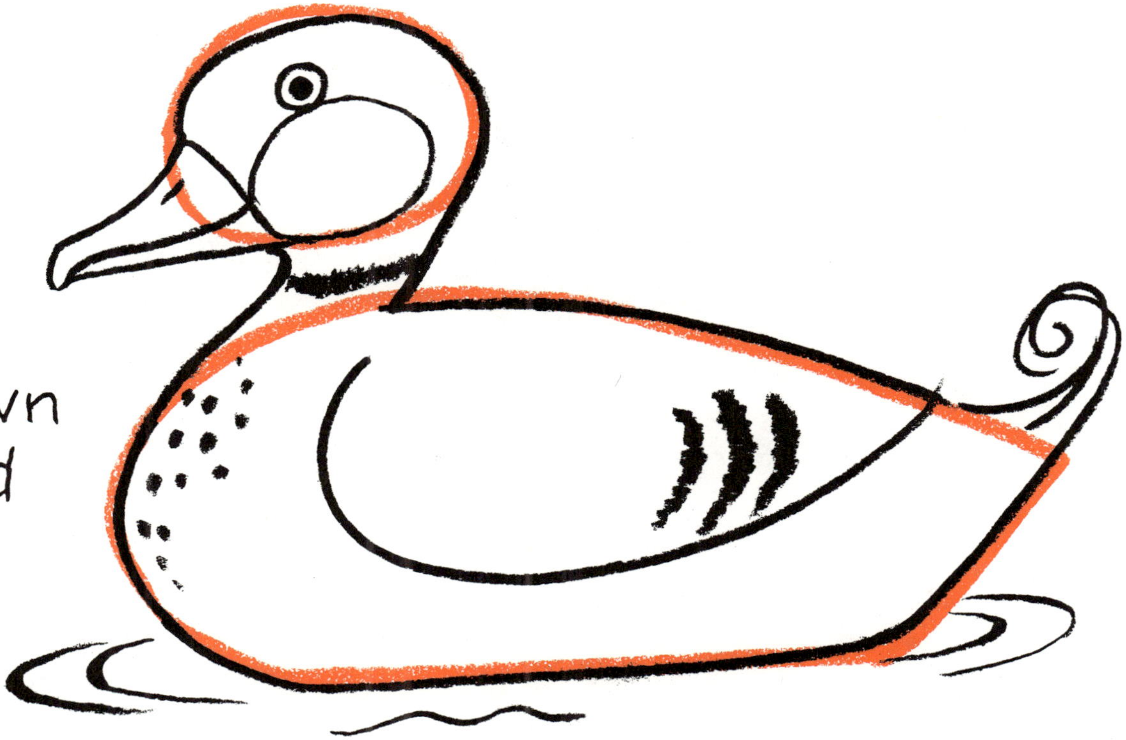

Sheep

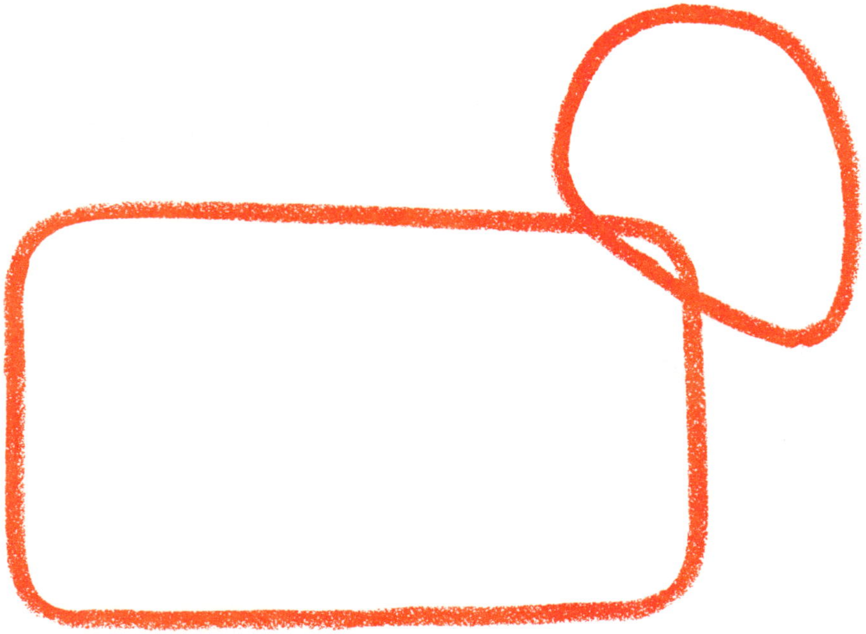

1. Draw these Two shapes.

Make a "woolly" look over forehead.

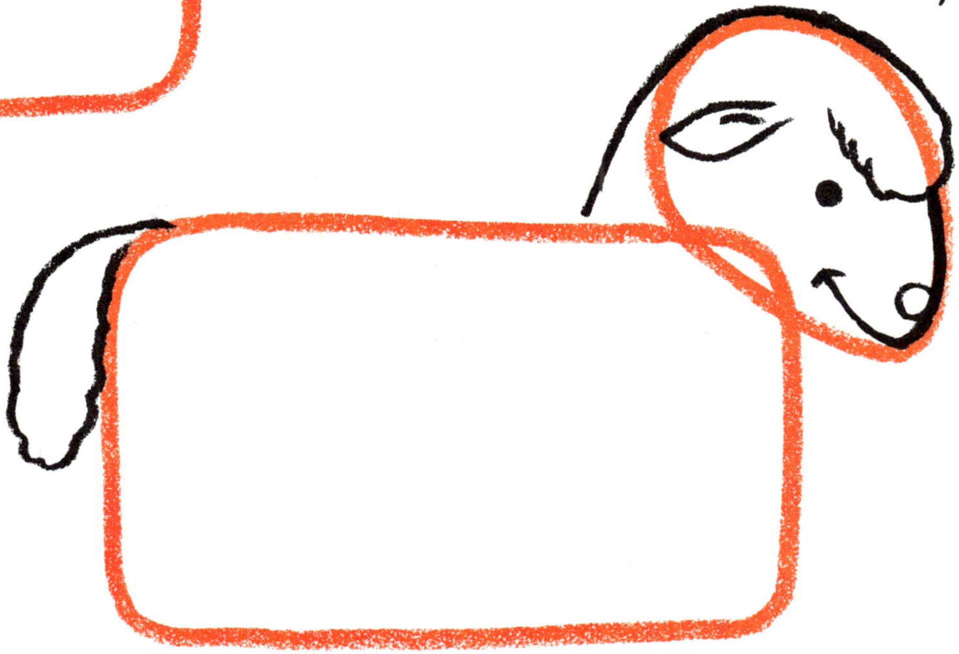

2. Add head with fuzzy top, and tail.

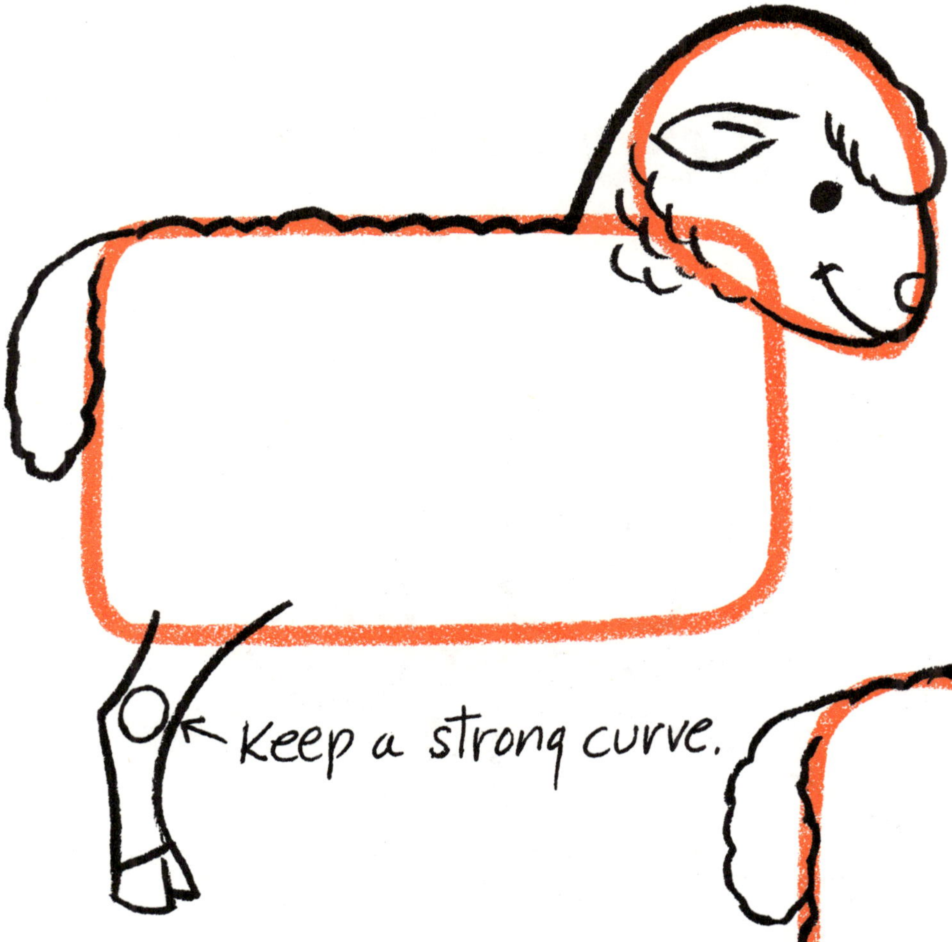

3. Add fluffy wool back and rear leg.

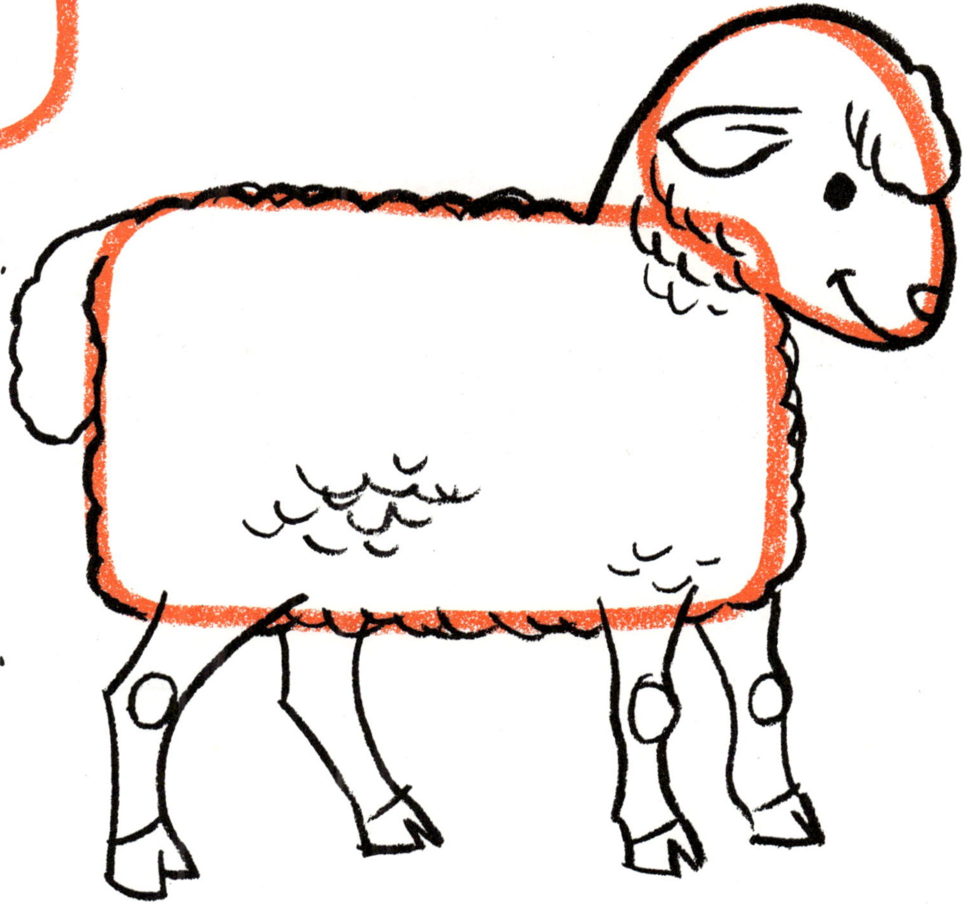

4. Finish the legs and the "woolly" body.

Koala Bears

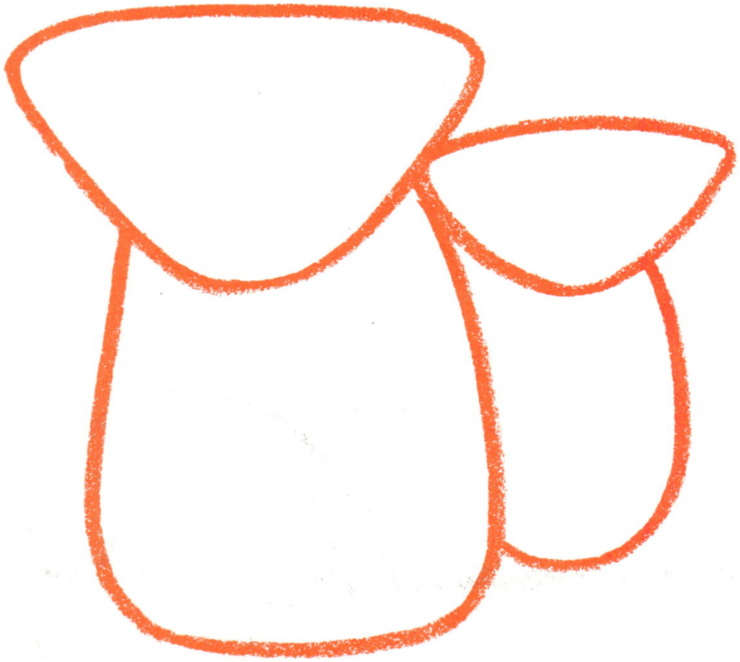

1. Draw two triangular and curved shapes.

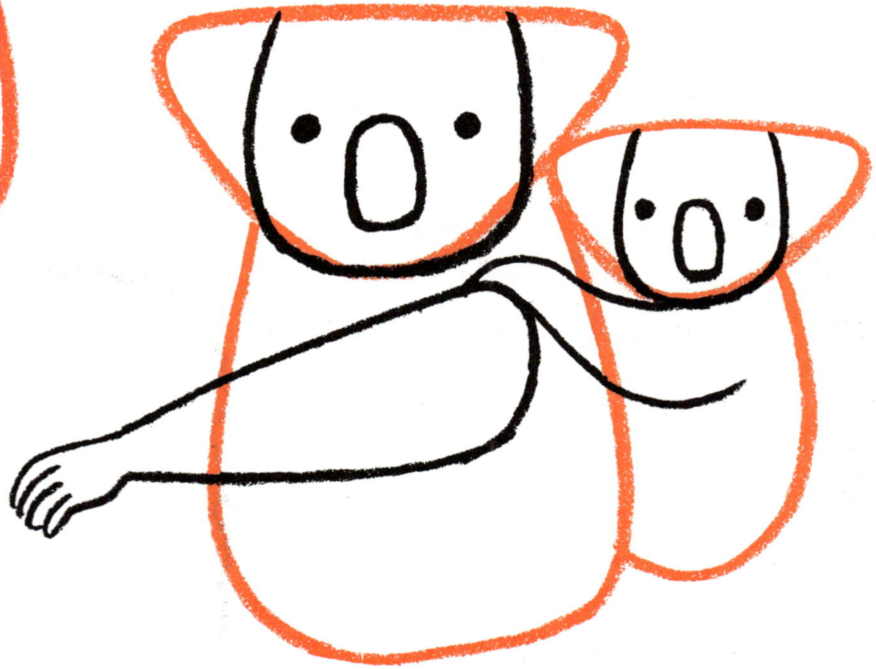

2. Add heads, eyes, noses and arms.

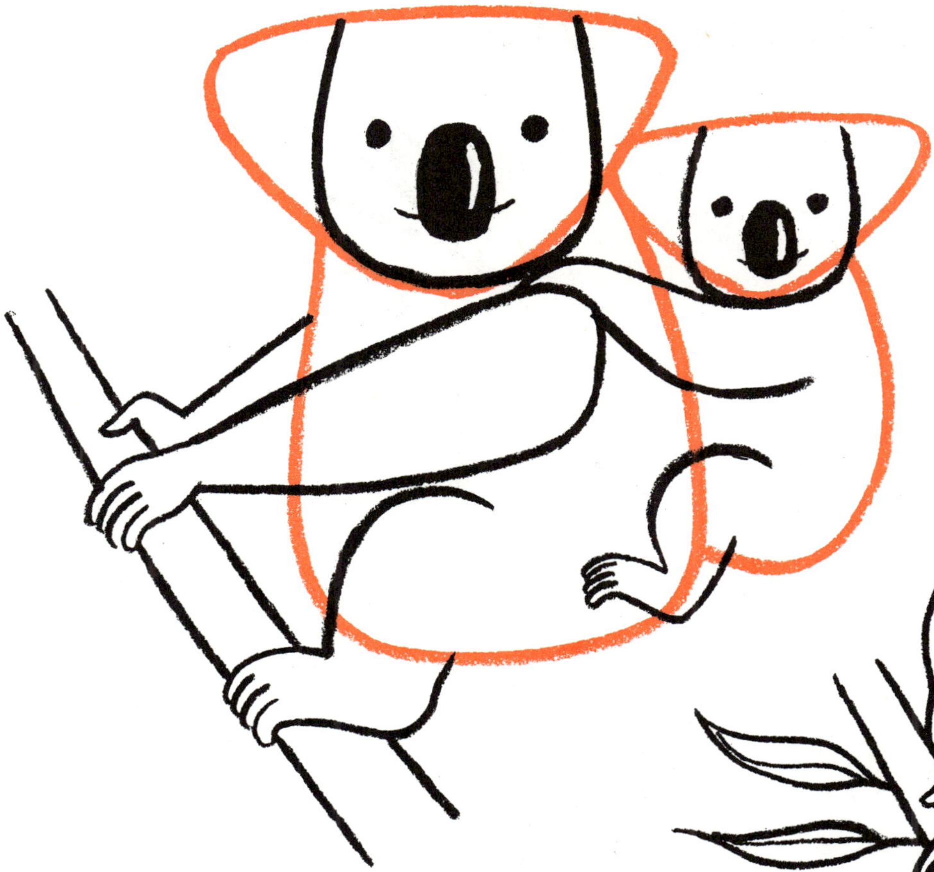

3. Draw the mama holding on to a tree limb. Finish the feet and mouths.

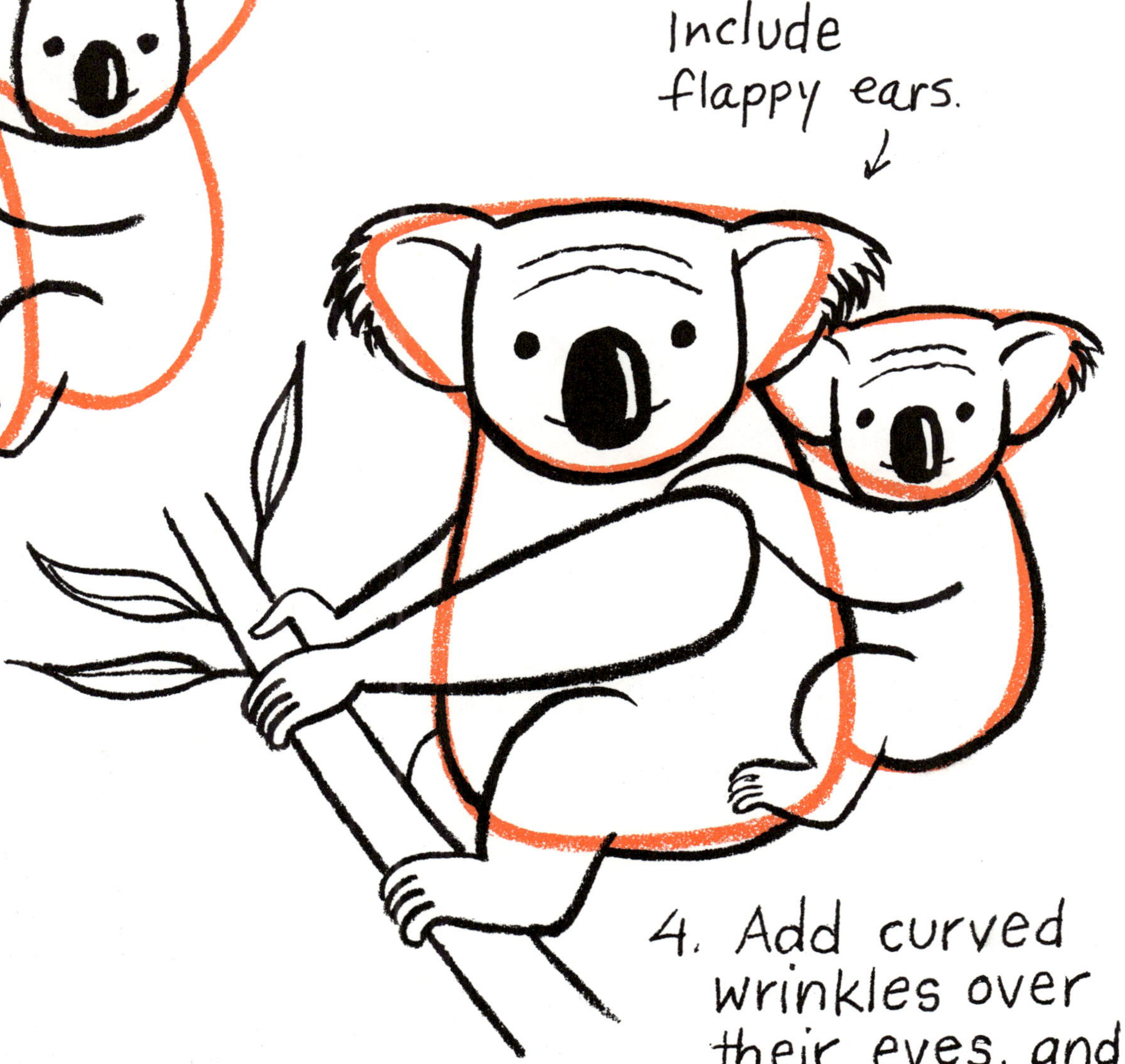

4. Add curved wrinkles over their eyes, and leaves on limb.

Kangaroo

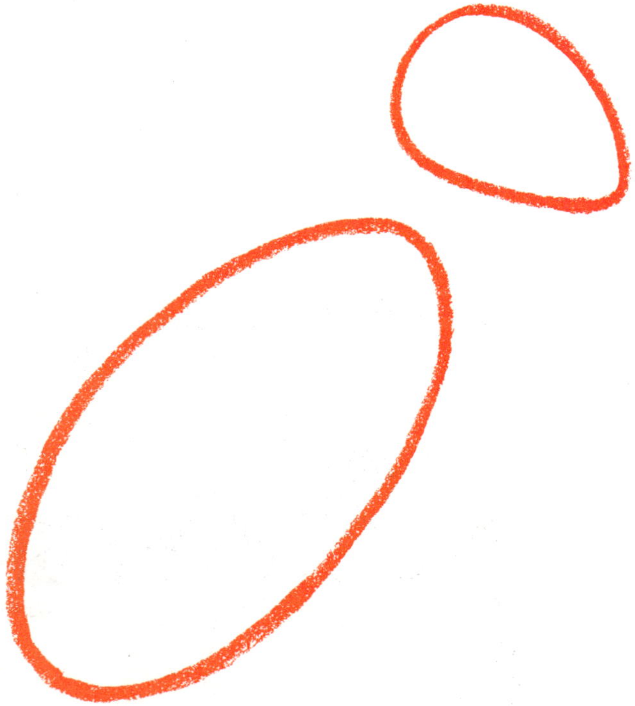

1. Draw these two shapes.

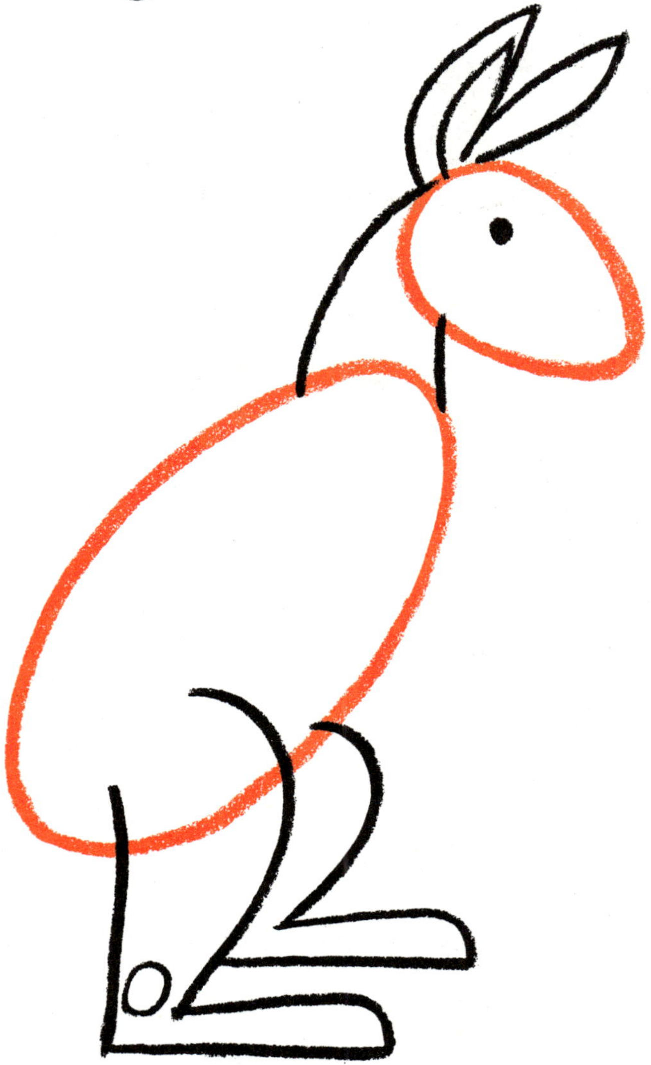

2. Add two strong jumper legs, neck, ears and eyes.

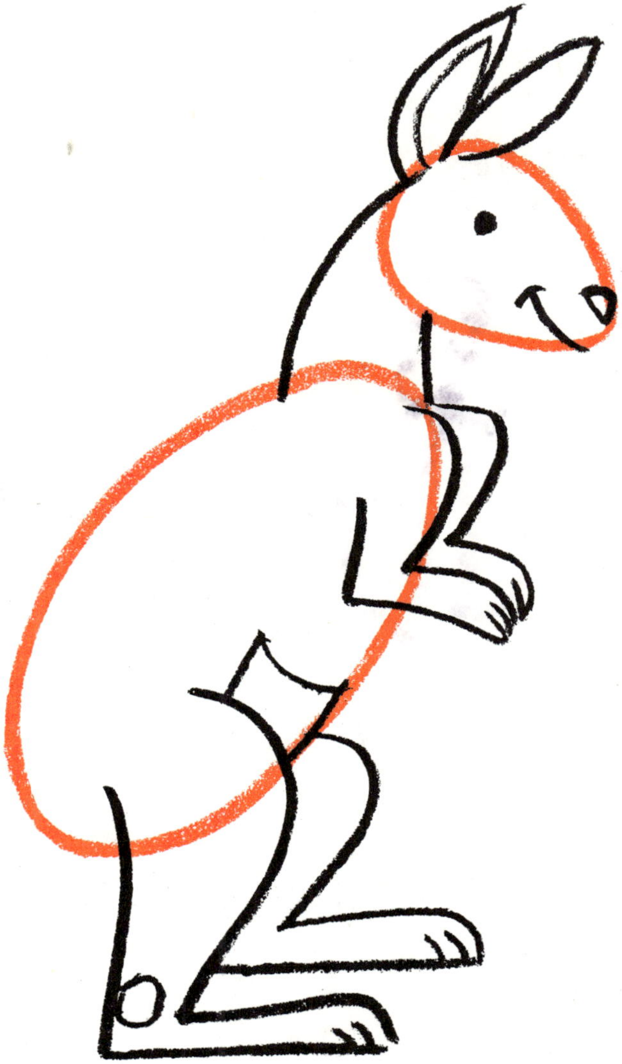

3. Draw two small arms and a pocket.

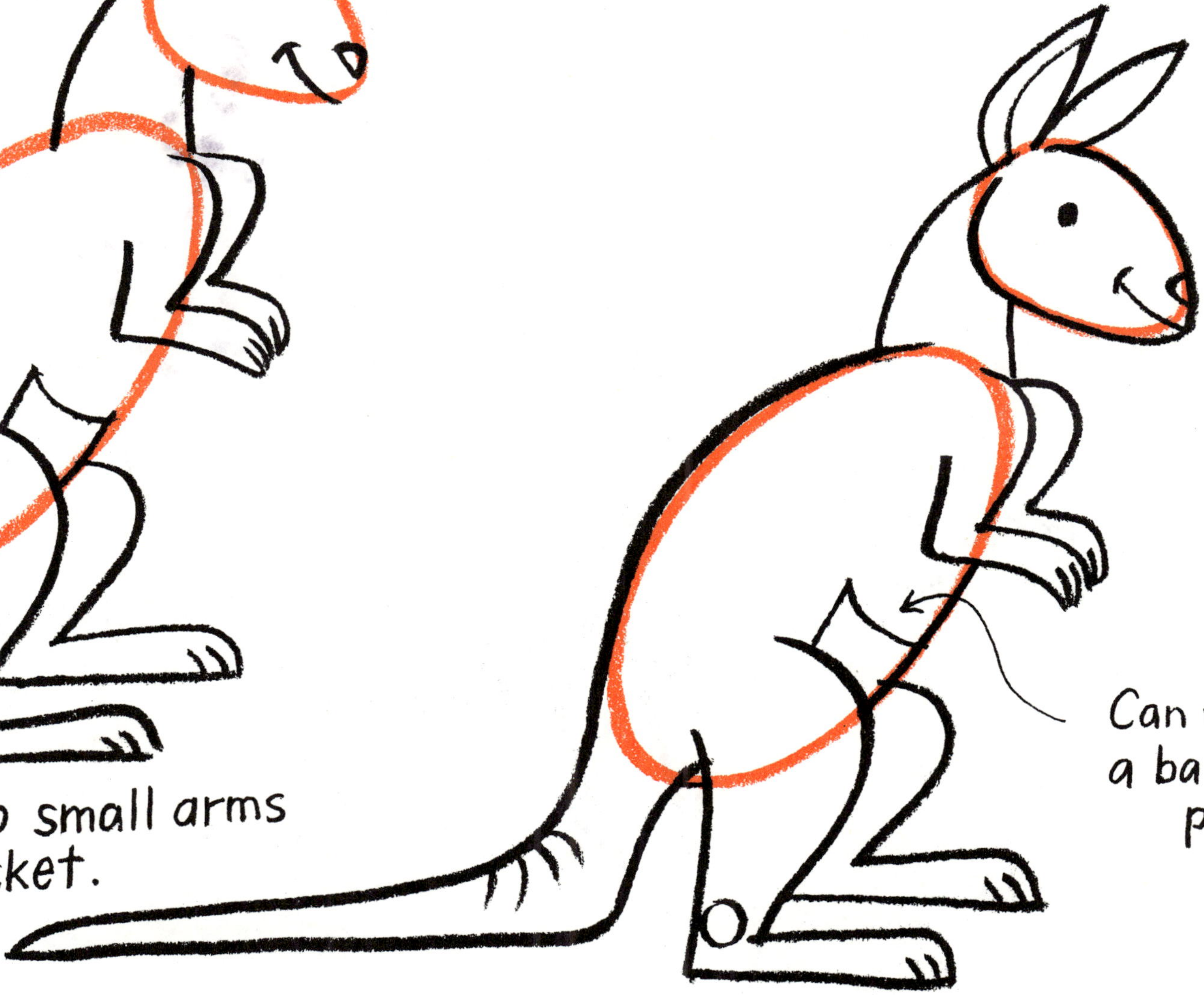

4. Finish with a huge tail.

Walrus

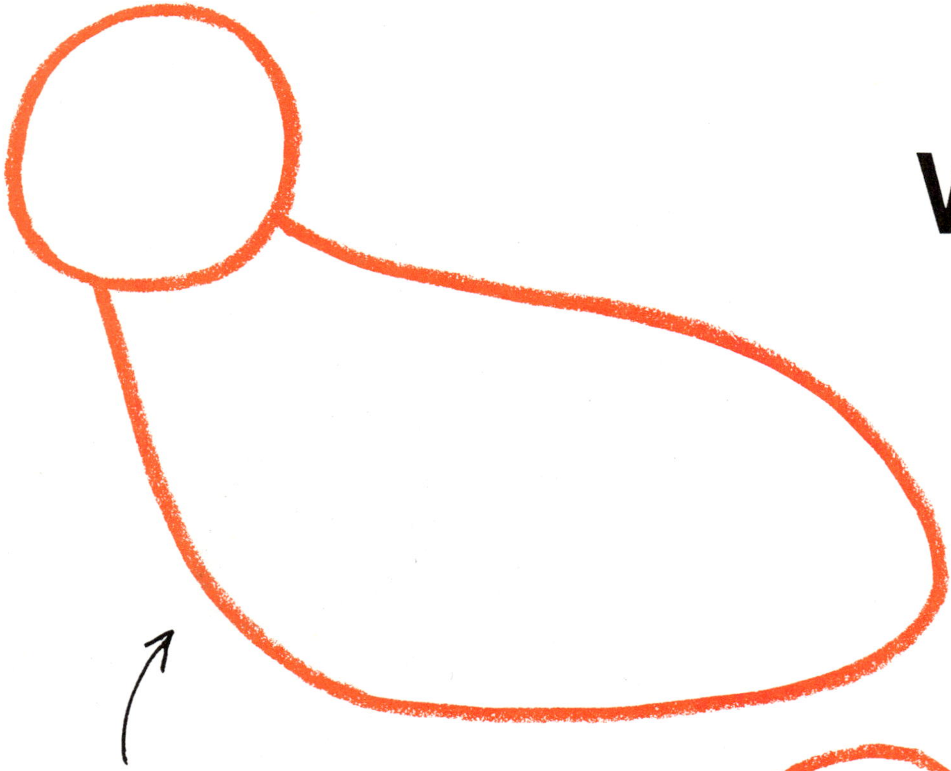

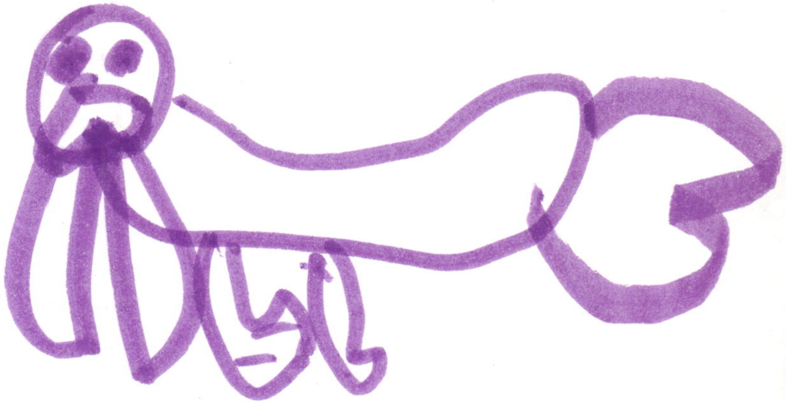

1. Draw a circle head and the body shape.

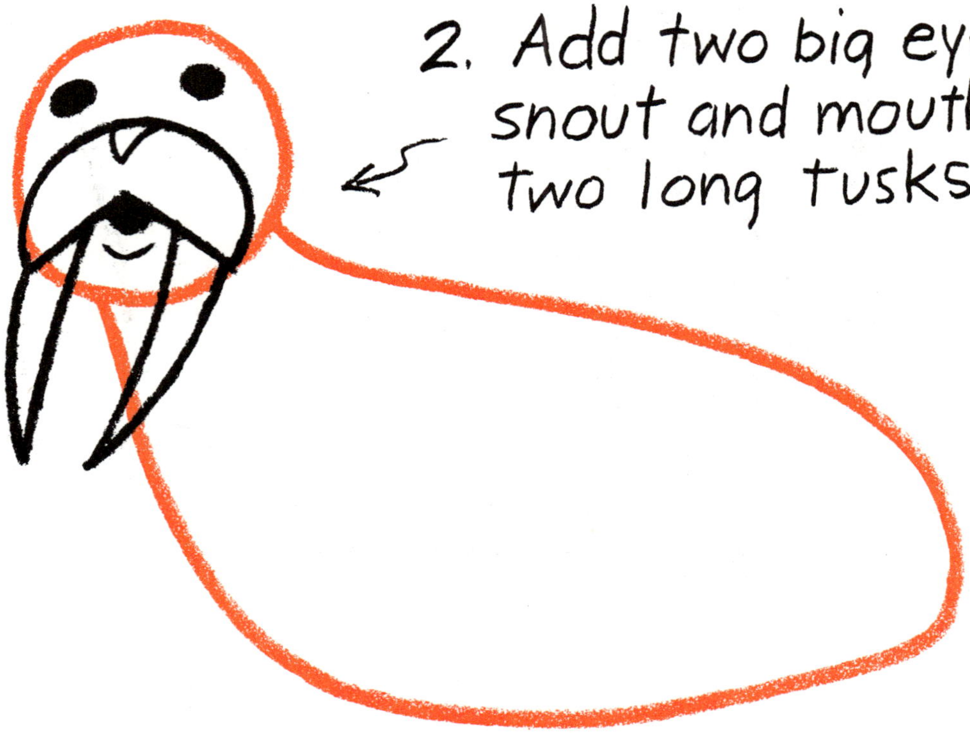

2. Add two big eyes, snout and mouth and two long tusks.

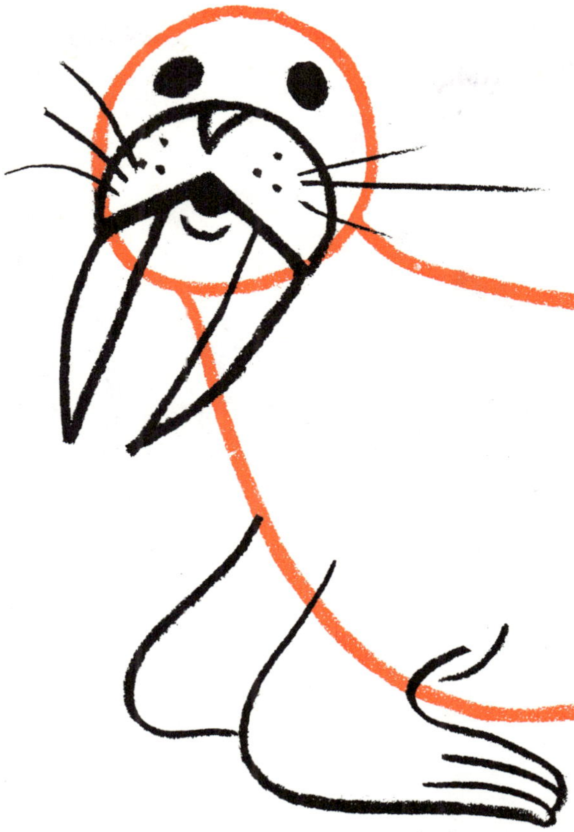

3. Draw front flippers.

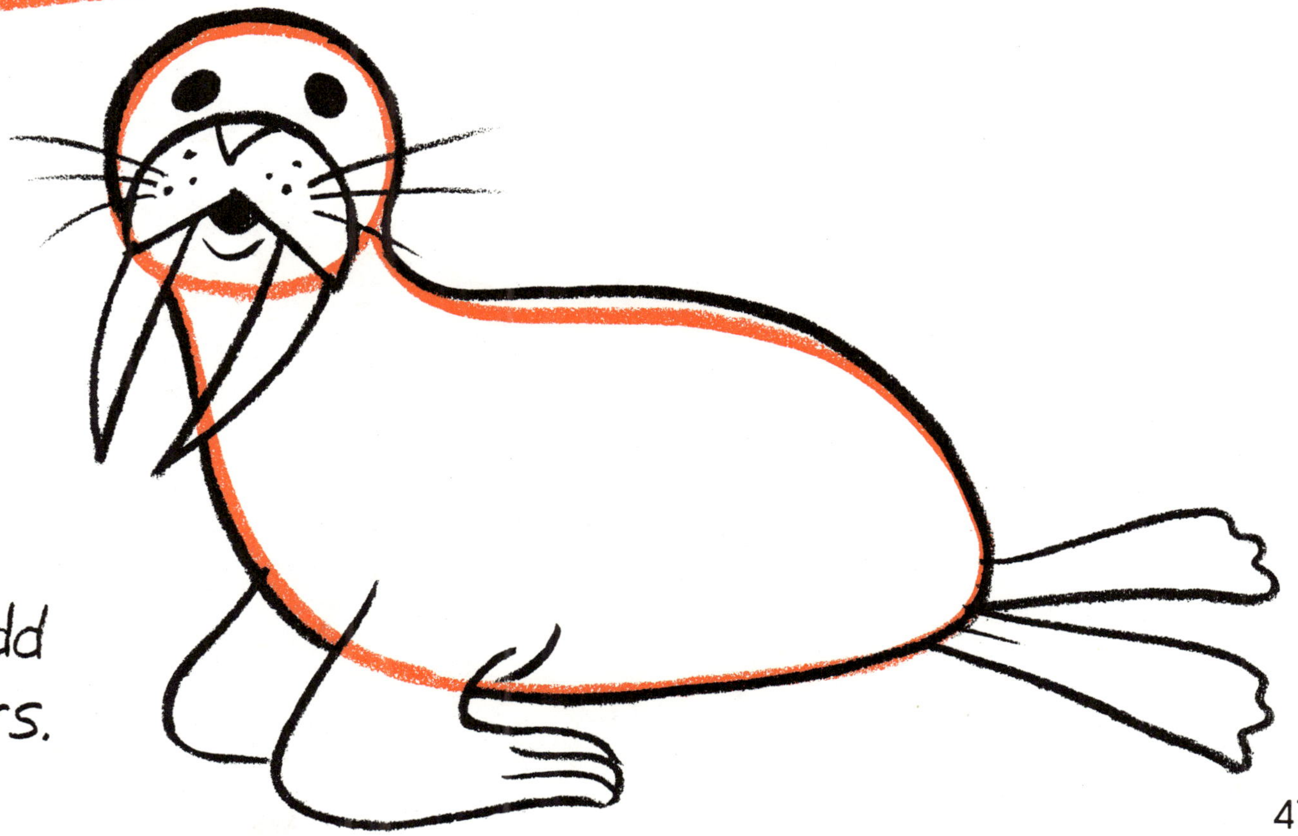

4. Finish his body and add rear flippers.

Hippopotamus

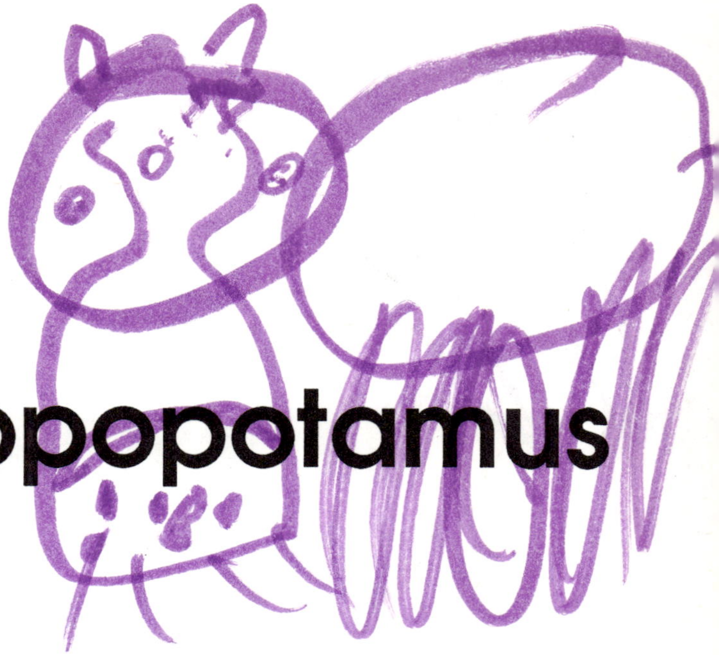

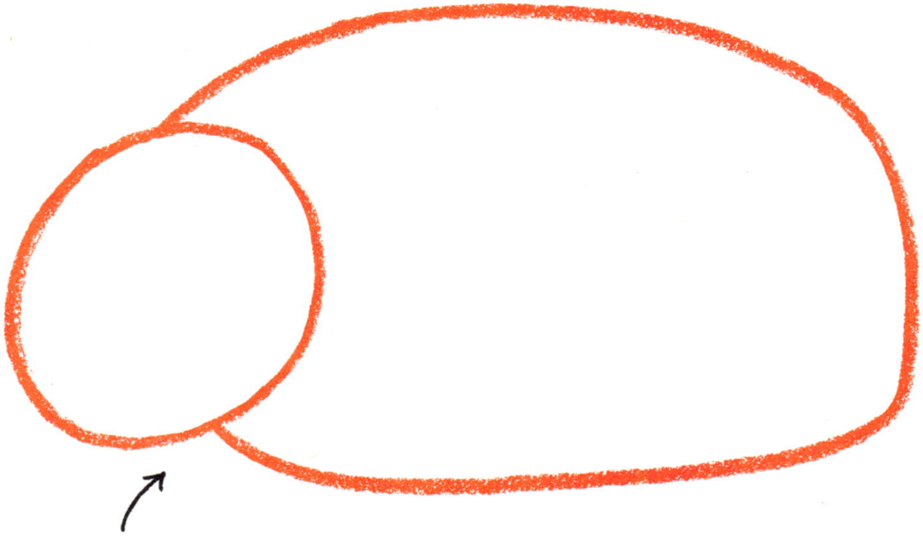

1. Start with these two shapes.

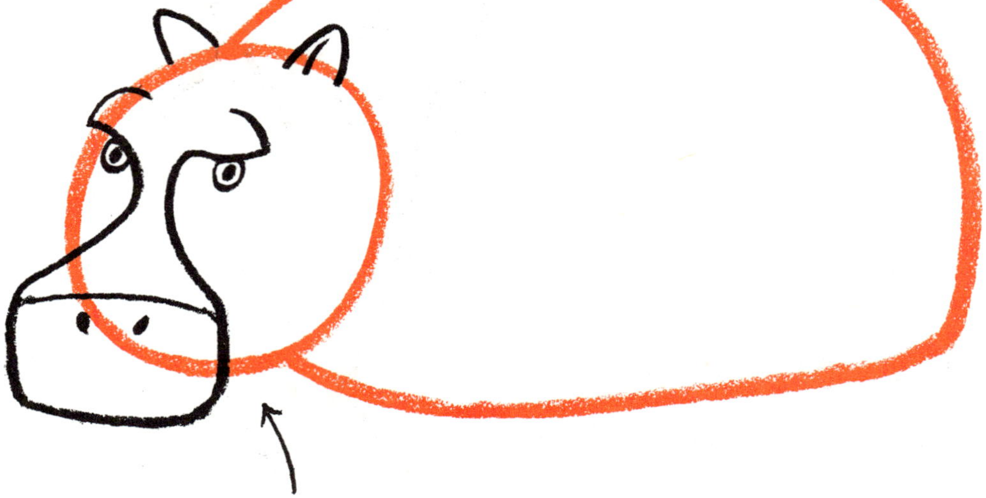

2. Draw huge nose, eyes and small ears.

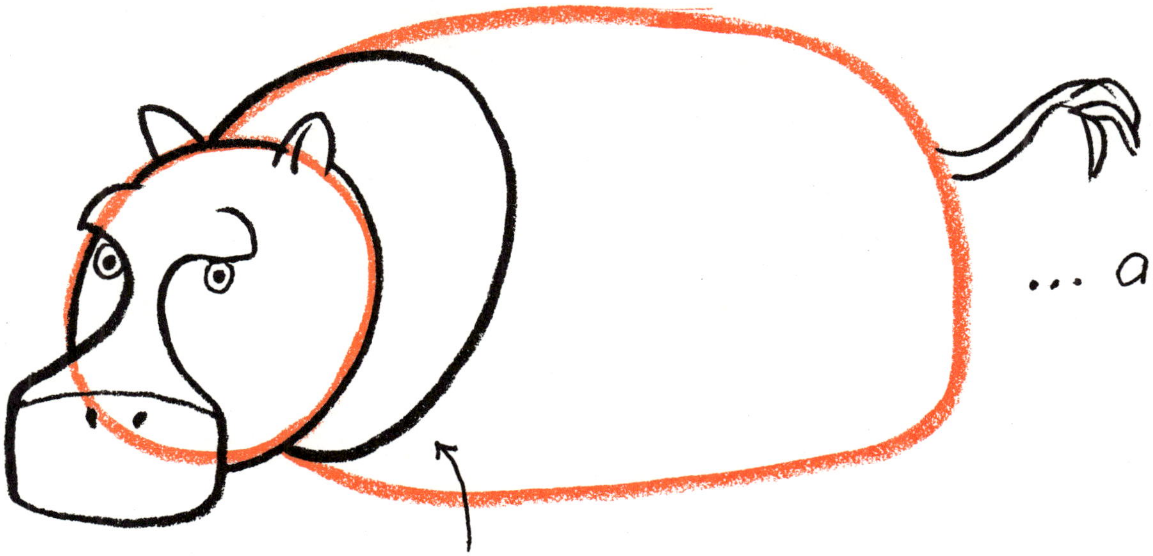

... and tail.

3. Add thick neck ...

4. Finish with whiskers and stubby legs.

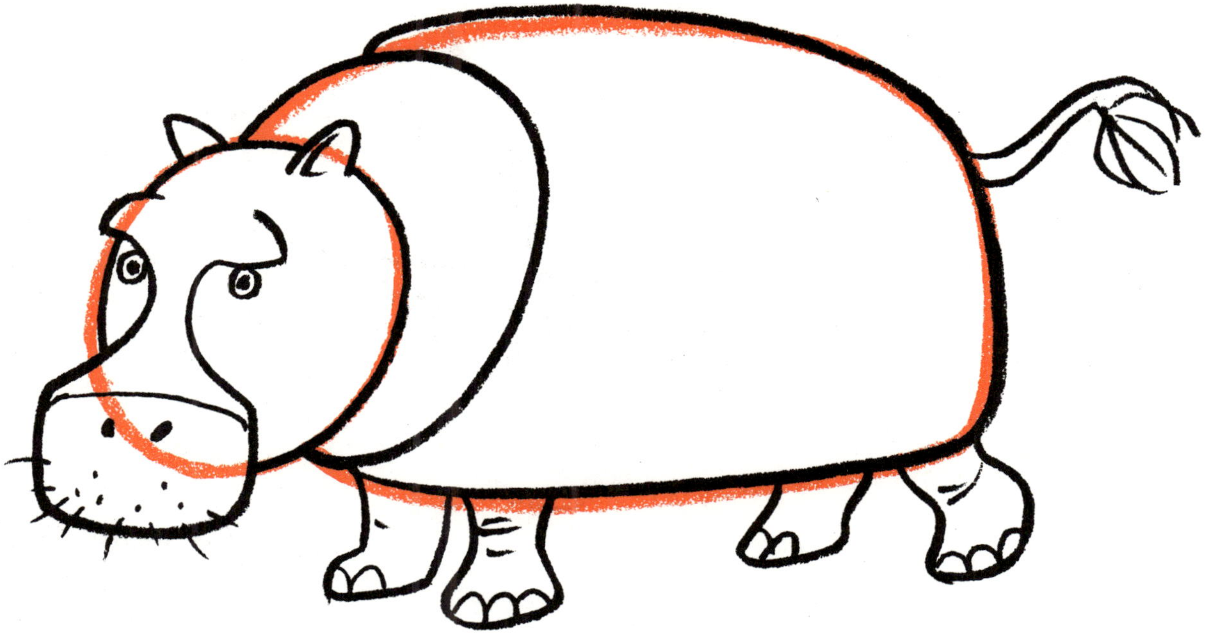

Elephant

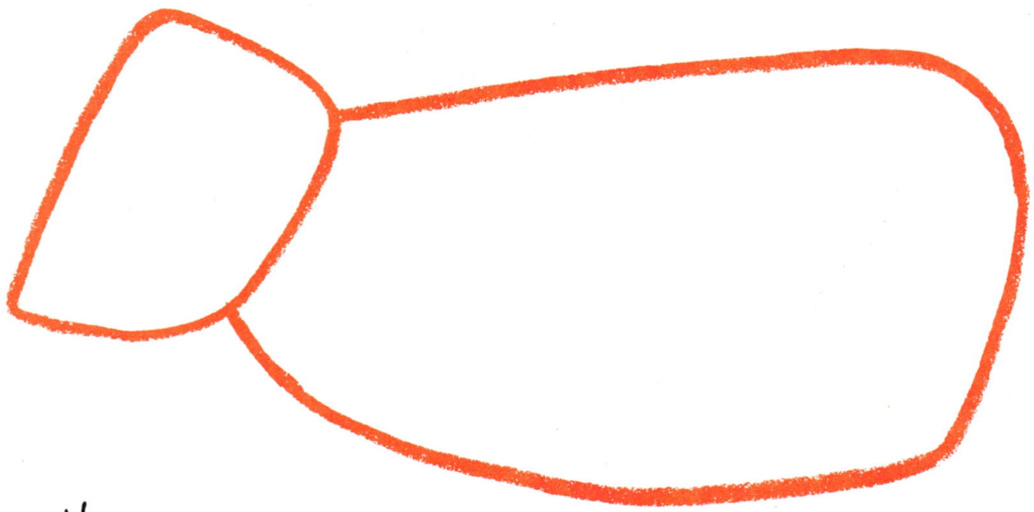

1. Draw these two shapes.

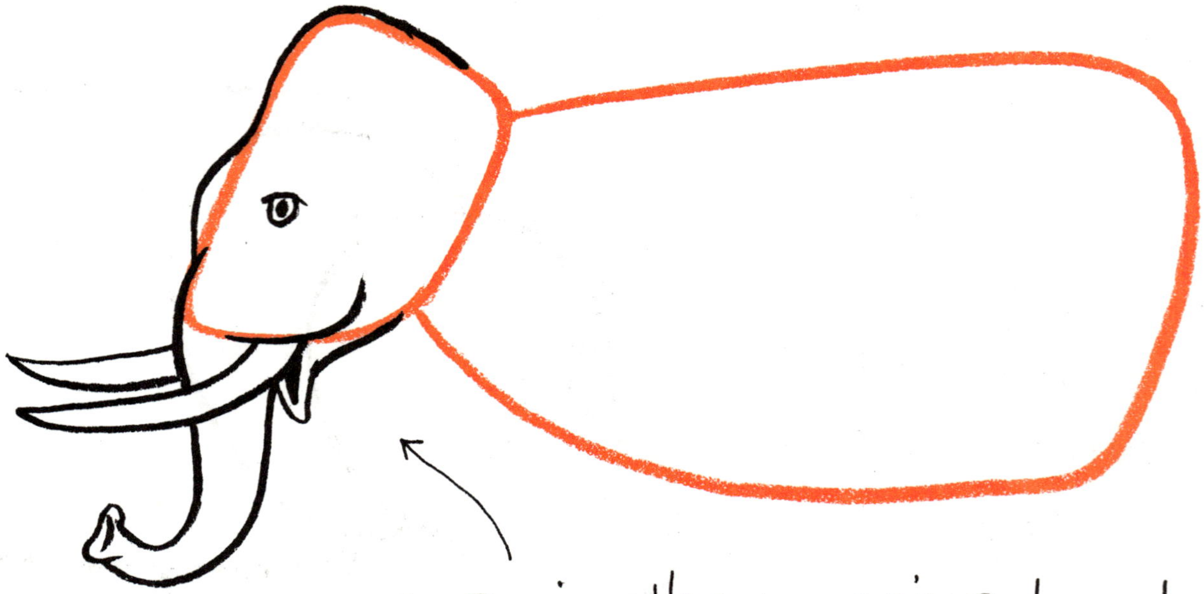

2. Begin the massive head, trunk, tusks, eye and mouth.

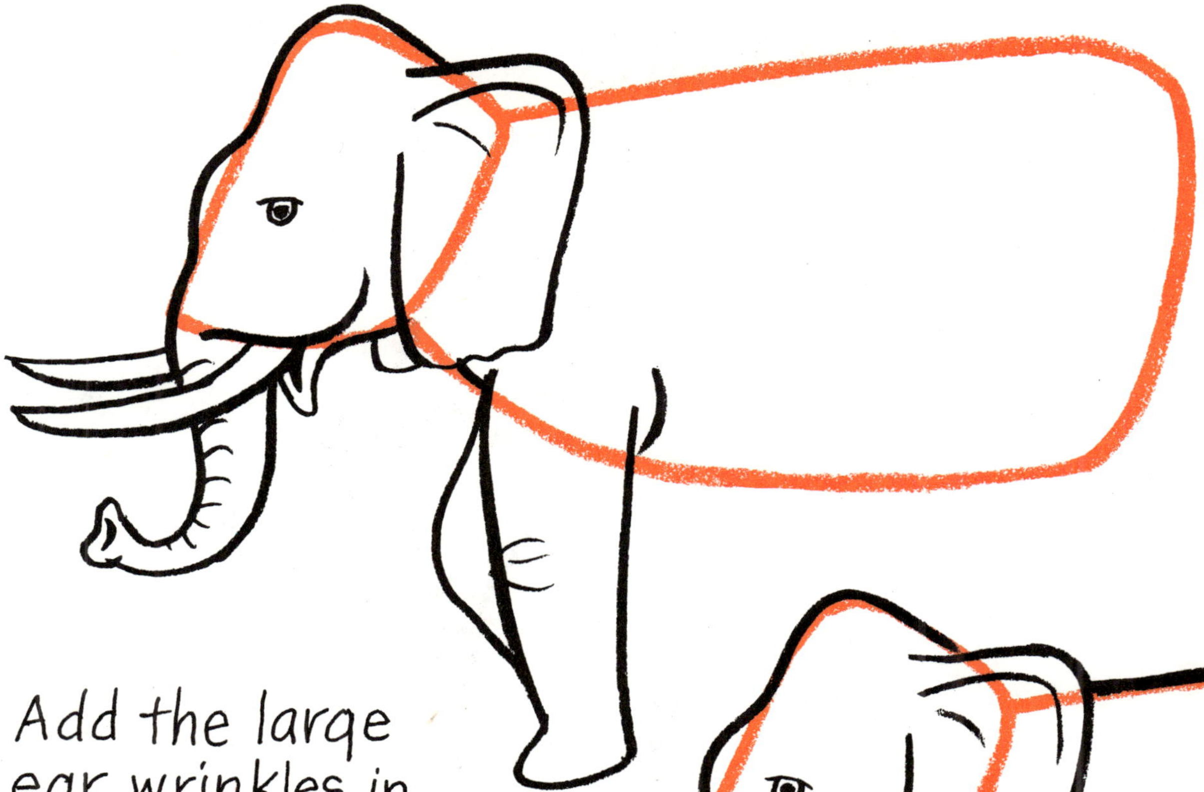

3. Add the large ear, wrinkles in trunk, and two front legs.

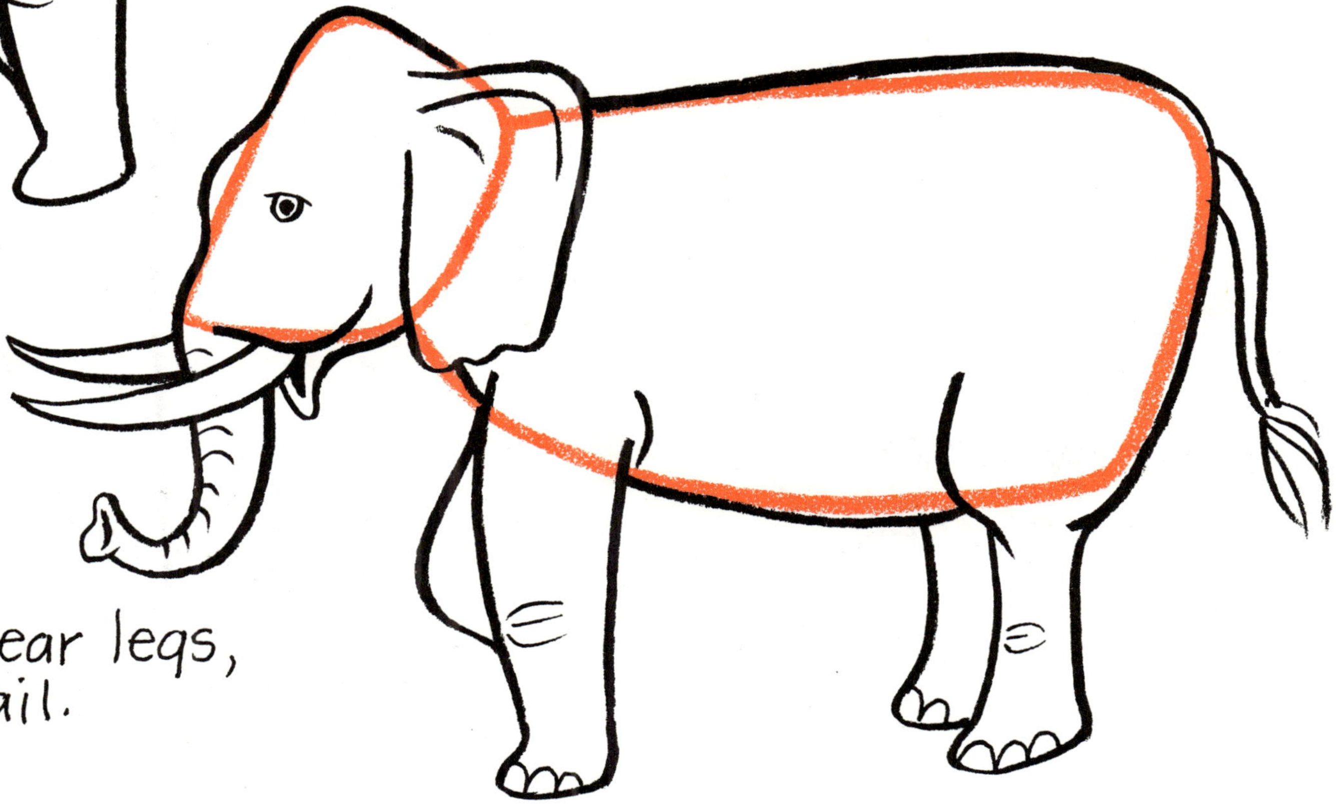

4. Finish body, rear legs, toenails and tail.

Gorilla

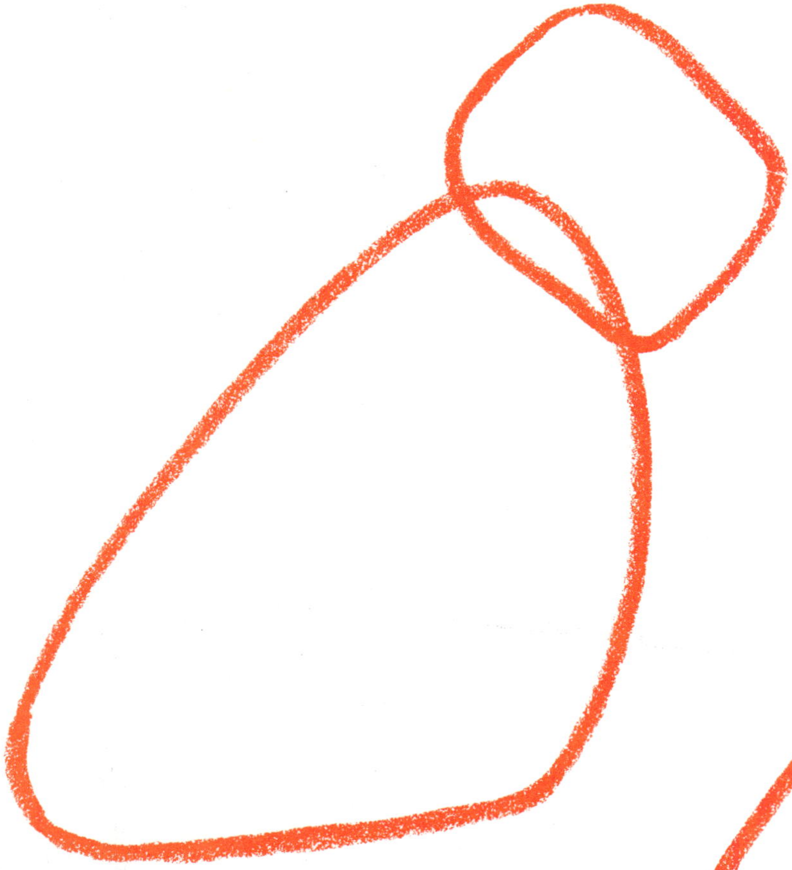

1. Draw these two shapes.

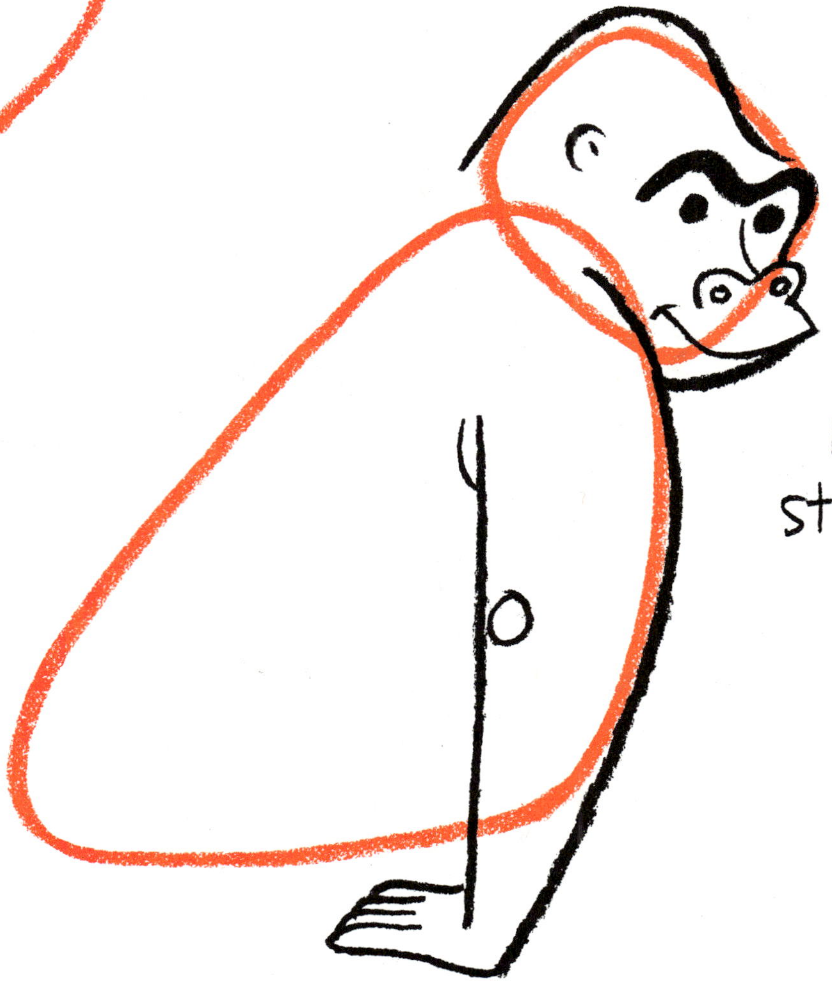

Make strong eyebrows.

2. Start head and arm.

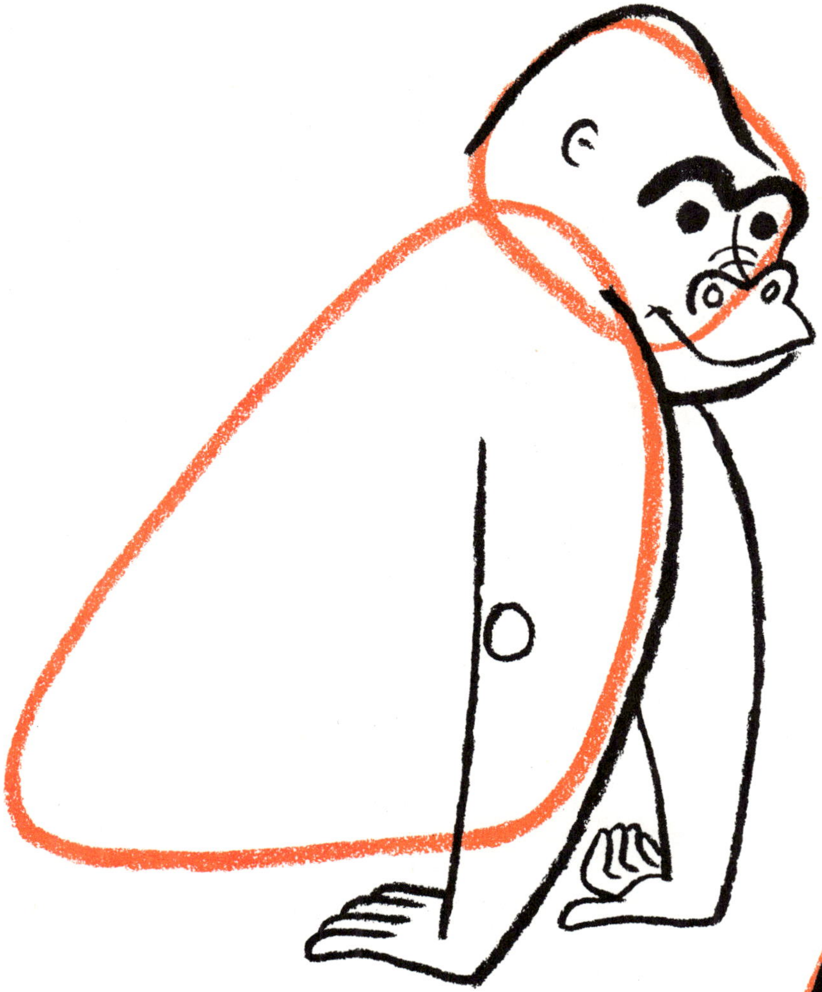

3. Draw other arm and fingers. Put wrinkles over nose.

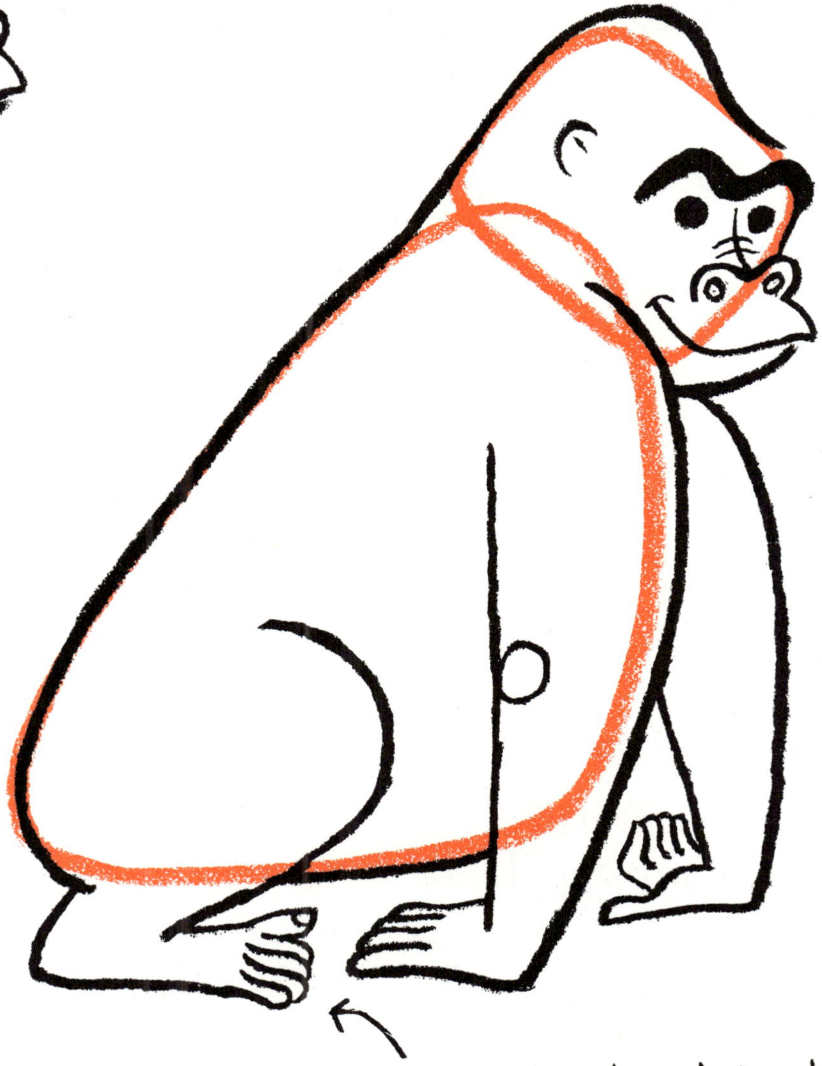

4. Finish with the hind leg.

Giraffe

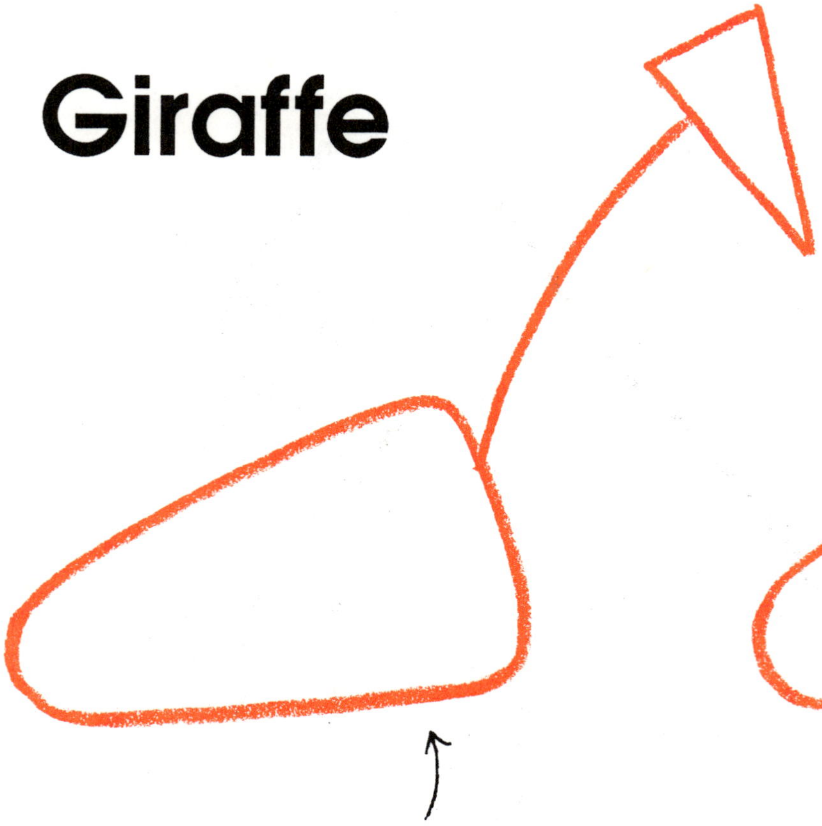

1, Draw these two shapes. Connect with a curved line.

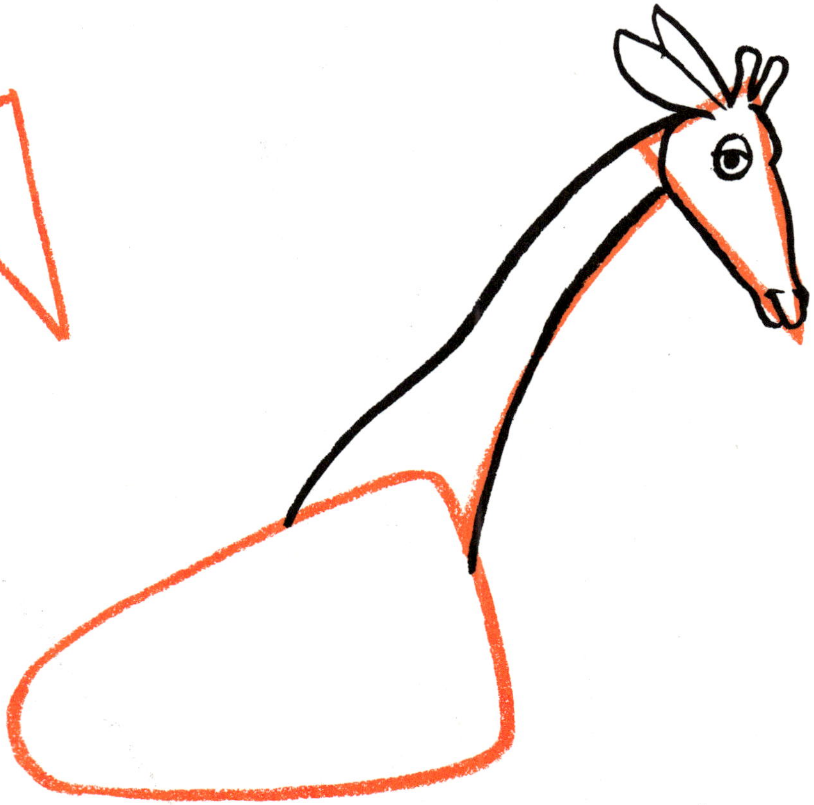

2. Complete the head and long neck.

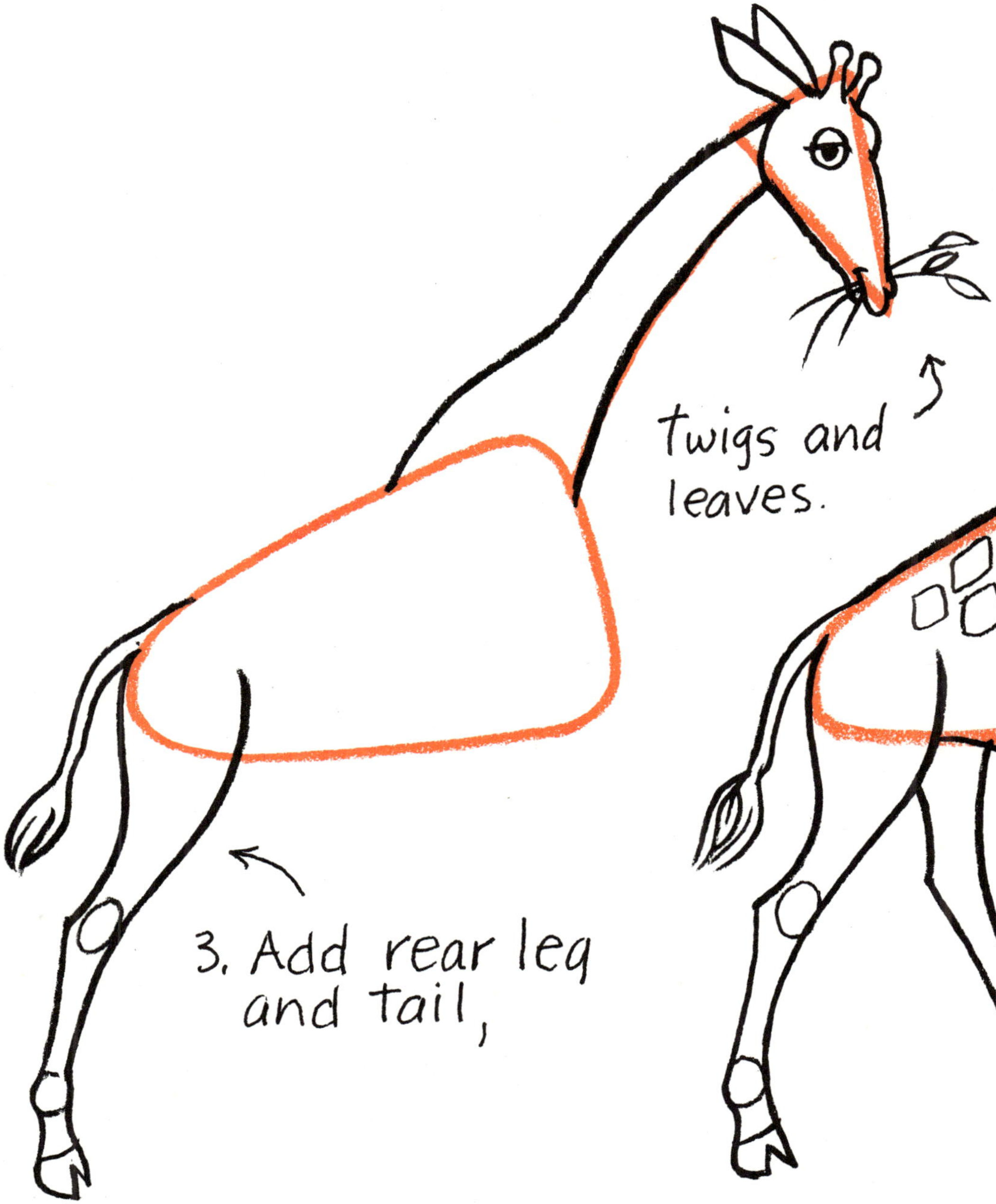

twigs and leaves.

3. Add rear leg and tail,

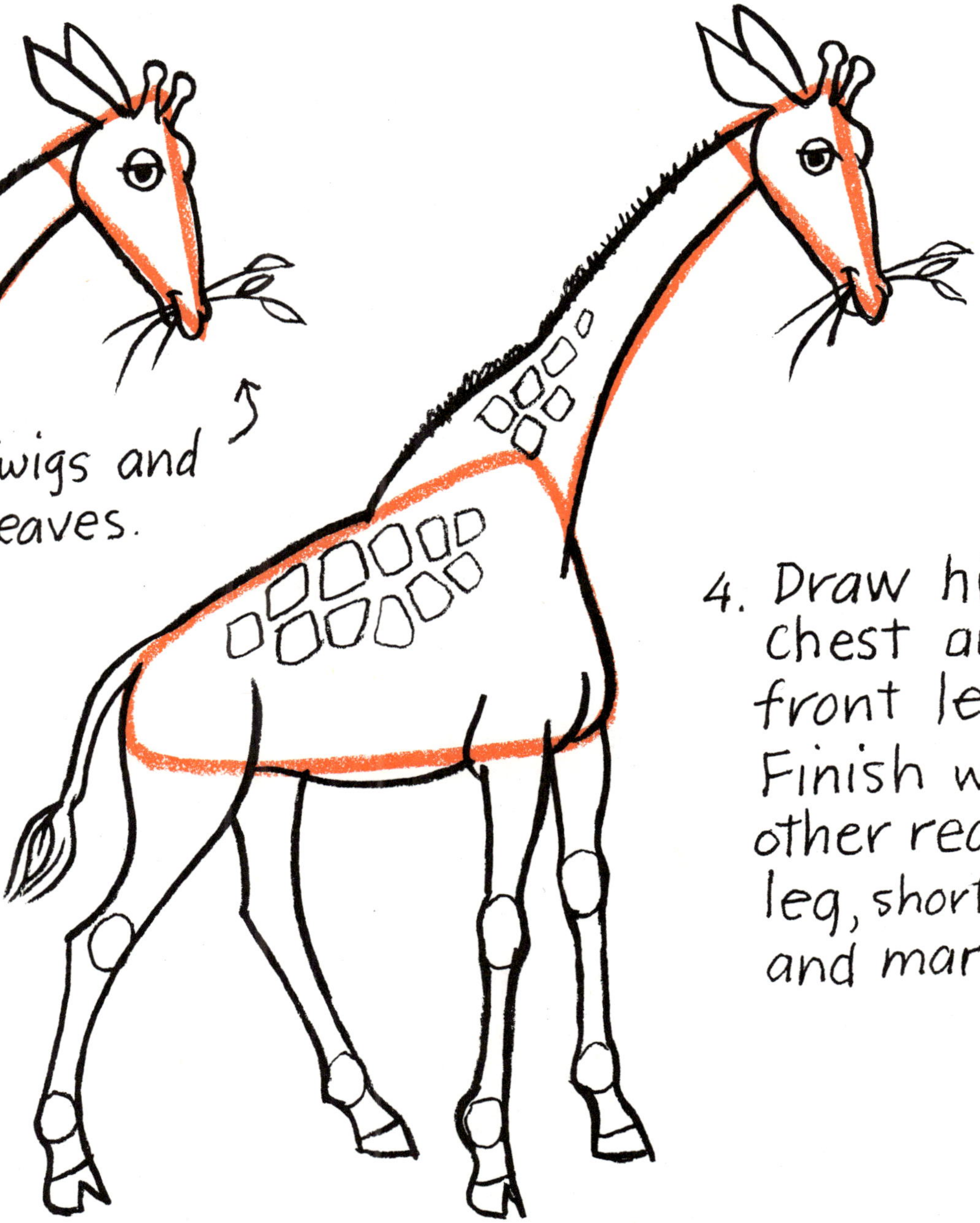

4. Draw his chest and front legs. Finish with other rear leg, short mane and markings.

Lion

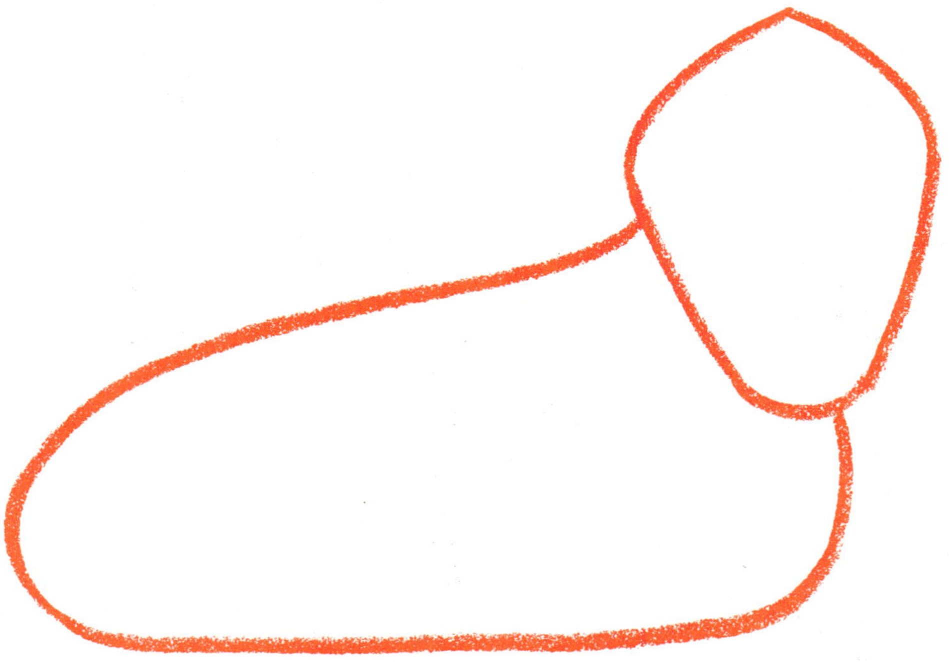

1. Draw these two shapes.

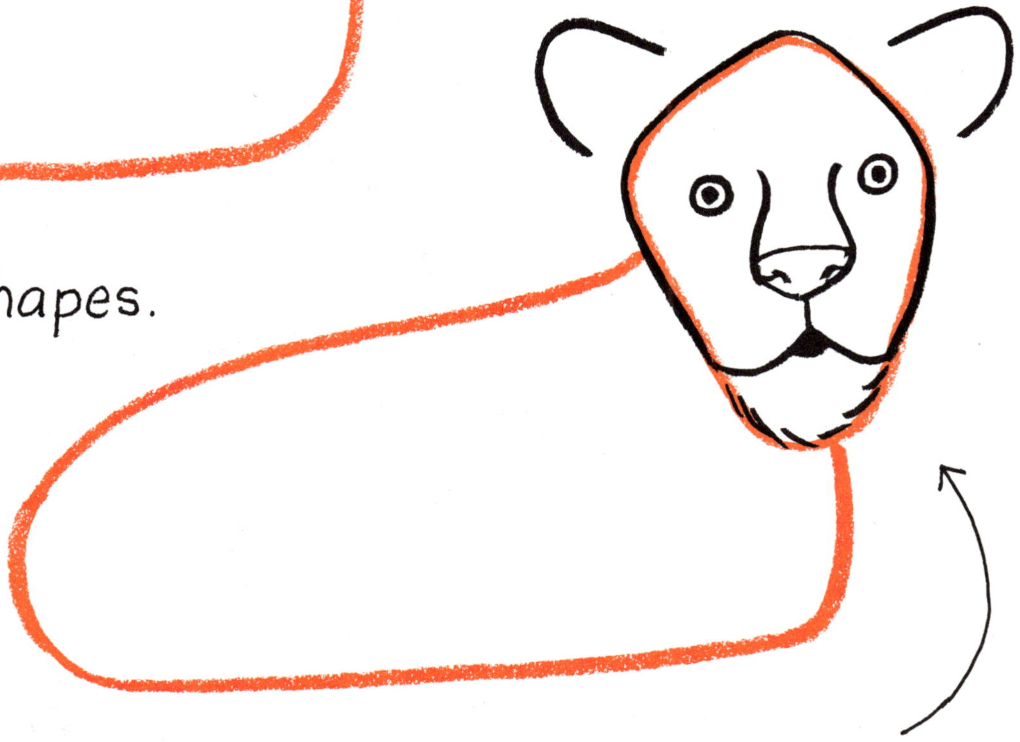

2. Add eyes, nose, ears and mouth.

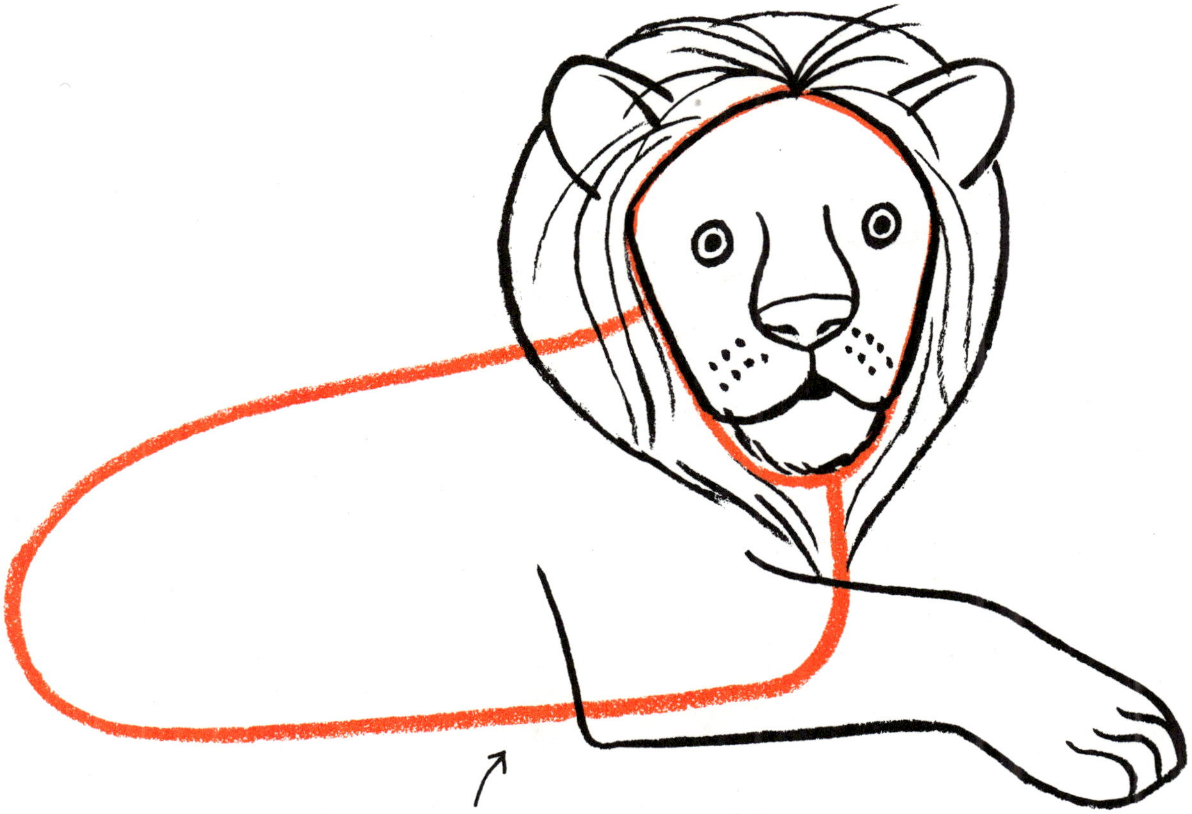

3. Draw large mane outline, then thin flowing hair strokes. Add large front leg and paw.

4. Finish eyes, and add whiskers. Draw other leg, body and tail.

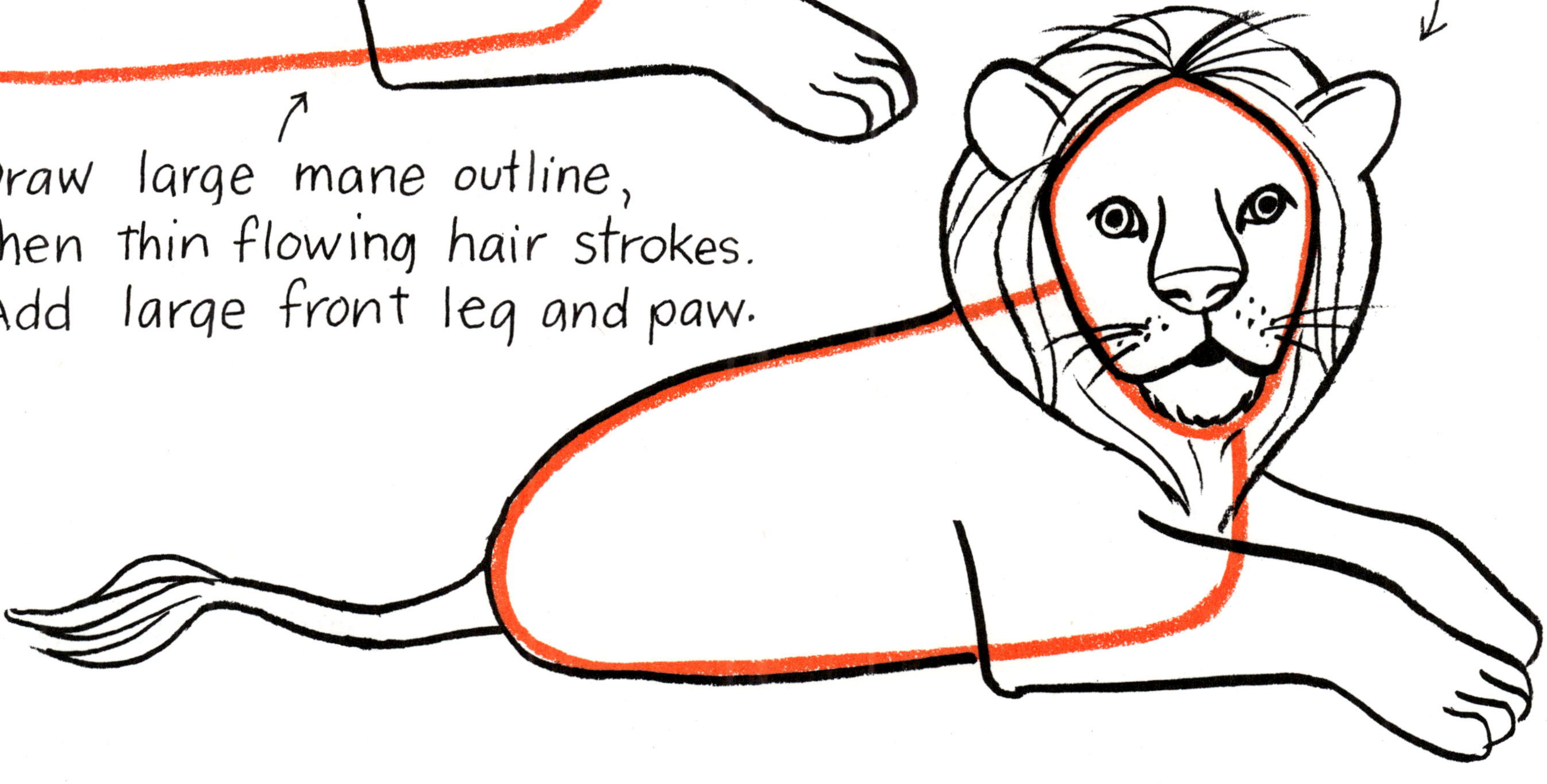

Dinosaur

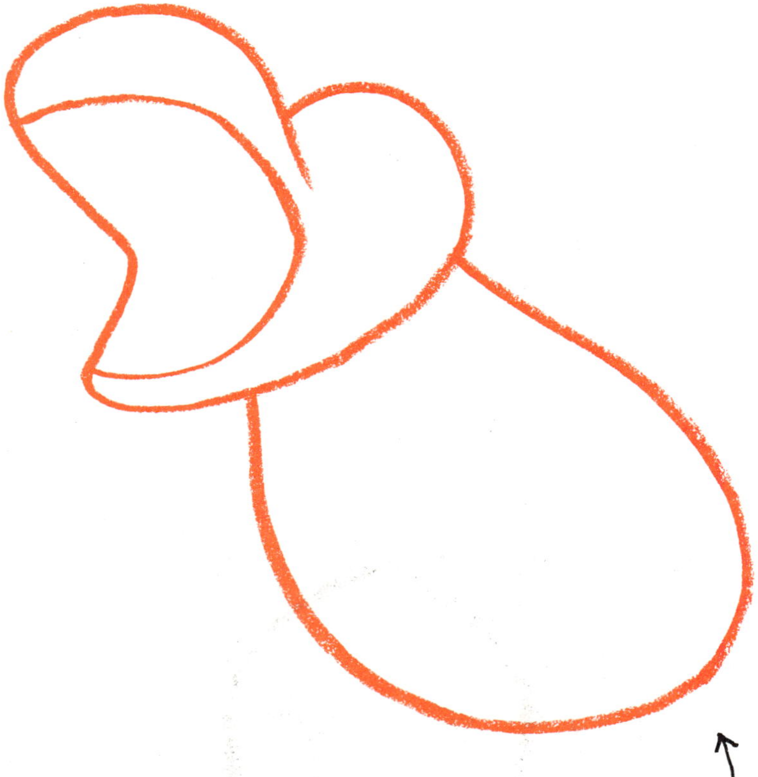

1. Start with these shapes.

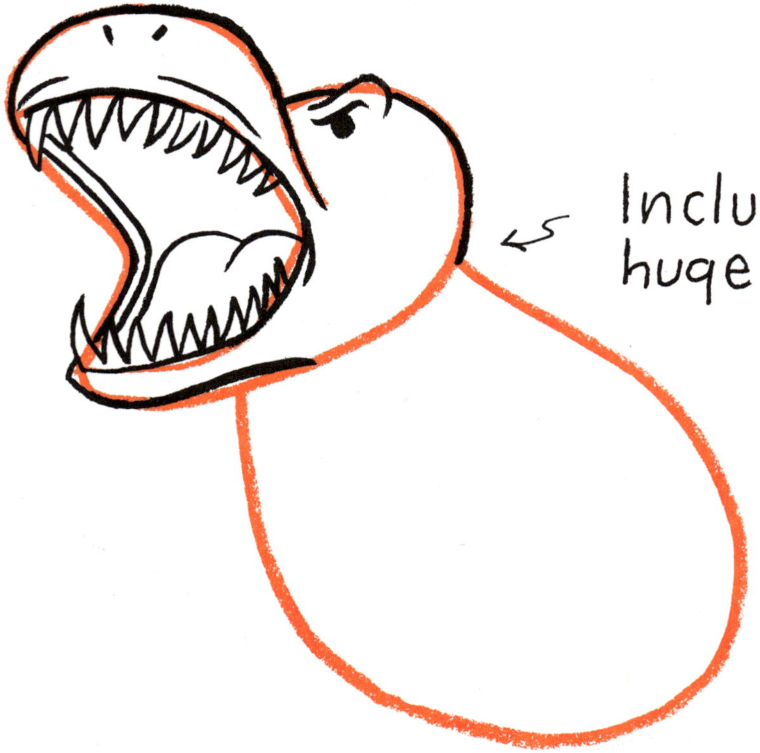

Include a huge tongue.

2. Add head, eye with "mean" look, and big open mouth with teeth.

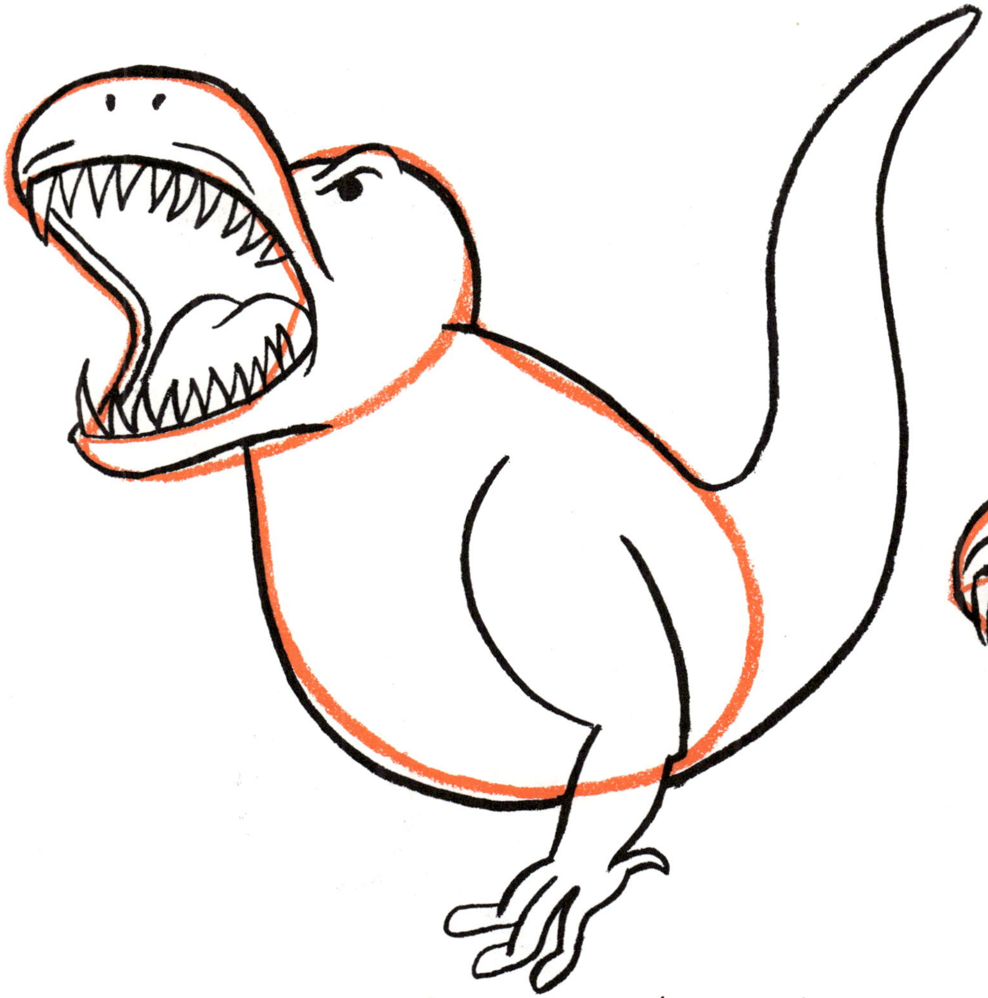

3. Draw body, leg and tail.

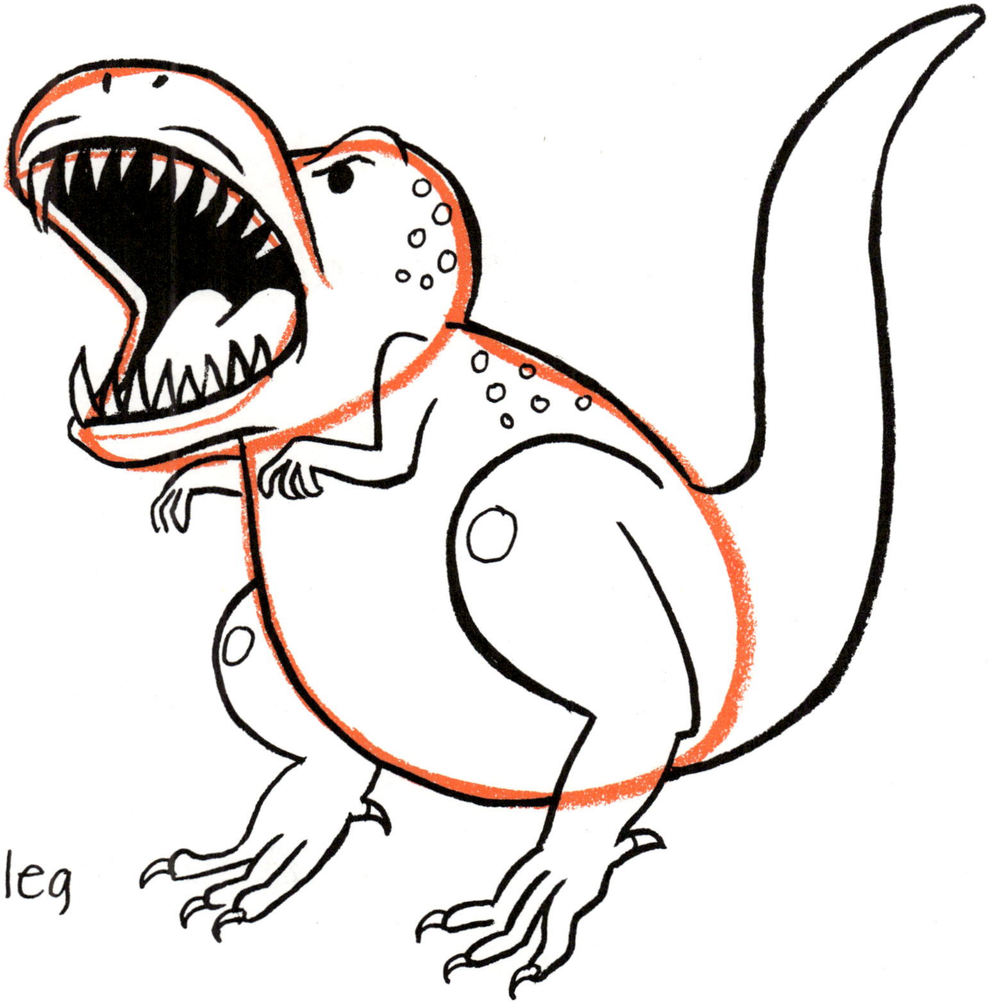

4. Finish with tiny arms, other leg and claws.

Horse

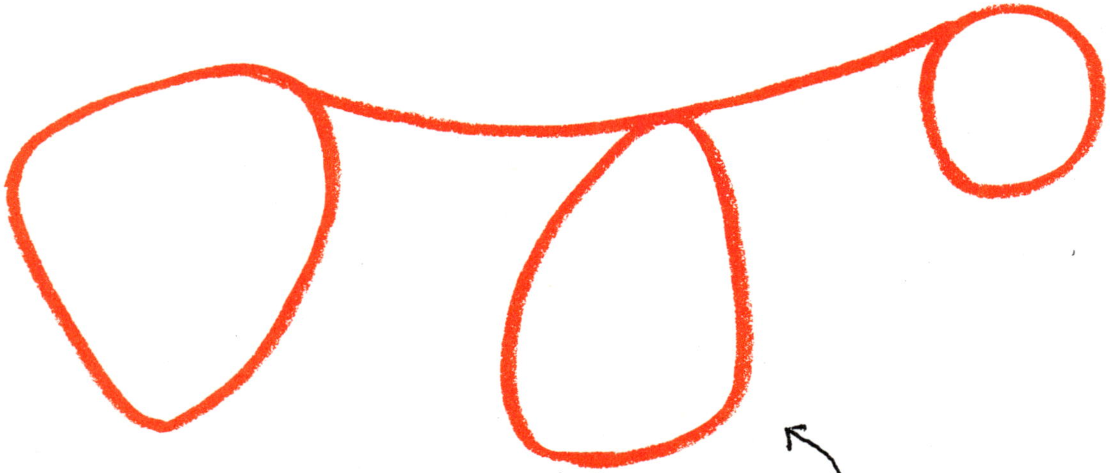

1. Start with these shapes.

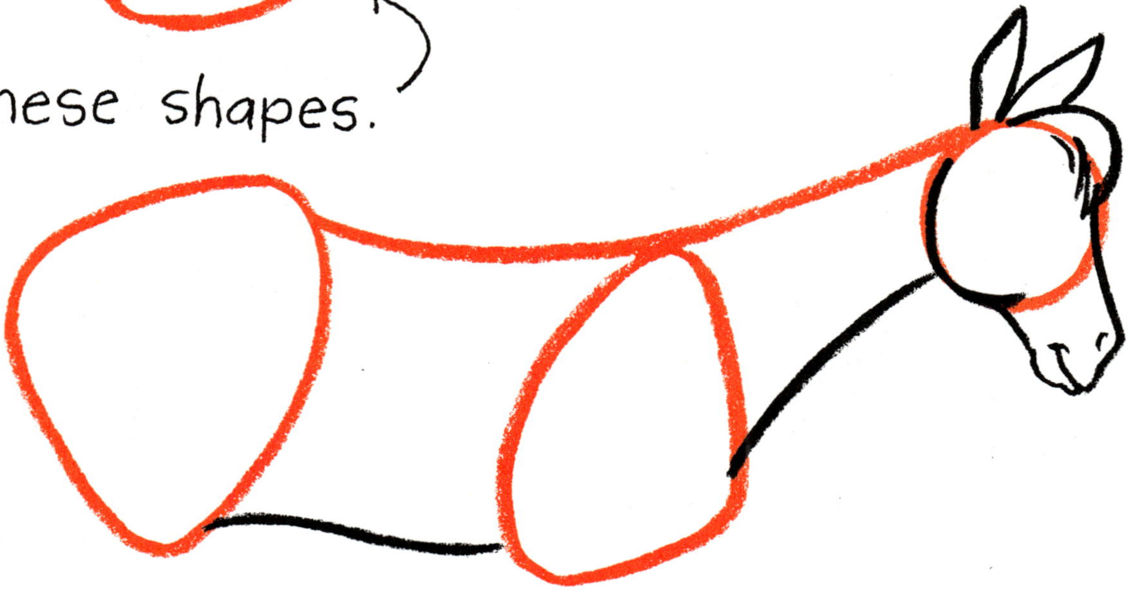

2. Add belly, neck and head.

Add powerful neck curve.

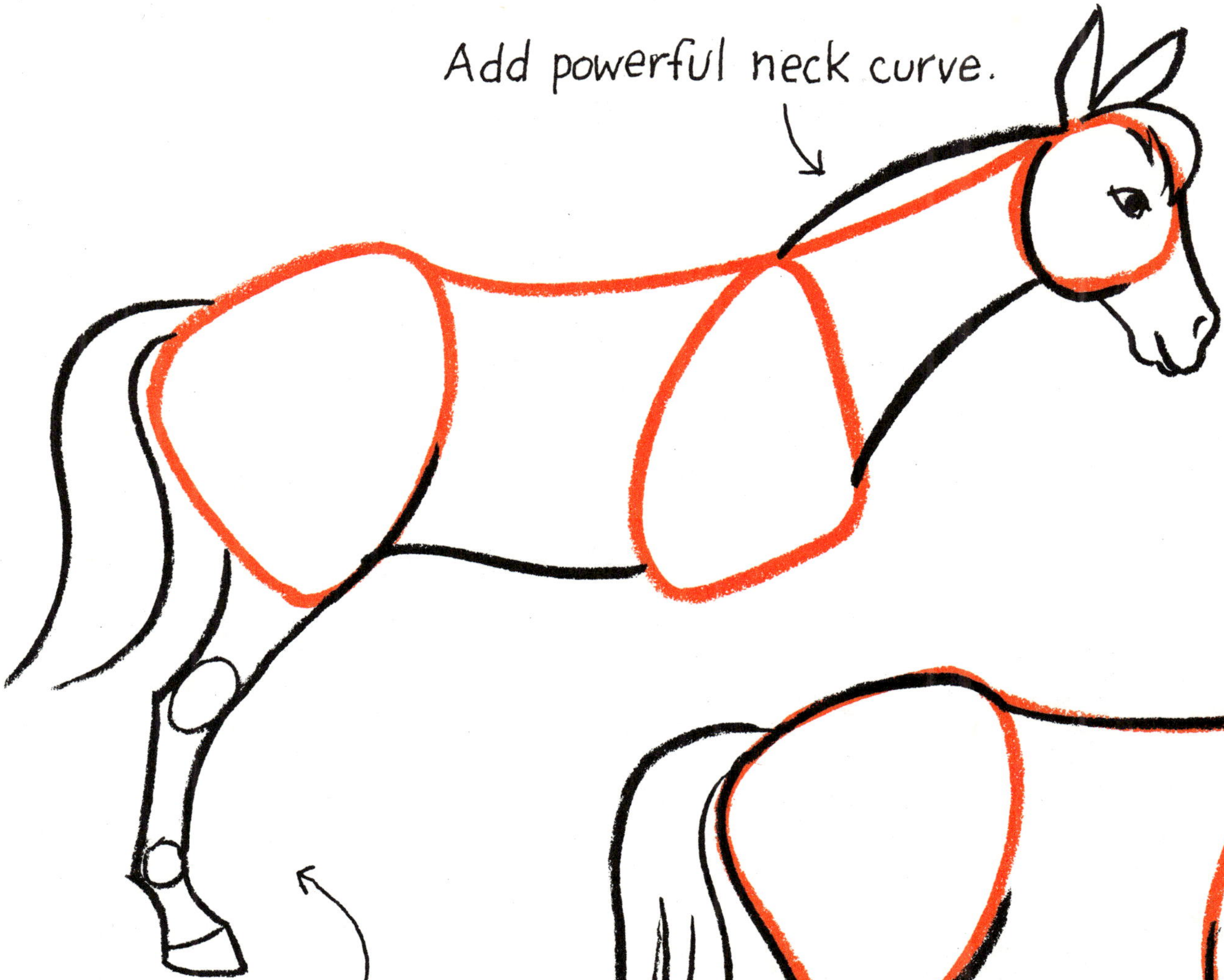

3. Start hind leg
and tail...
...including joints.

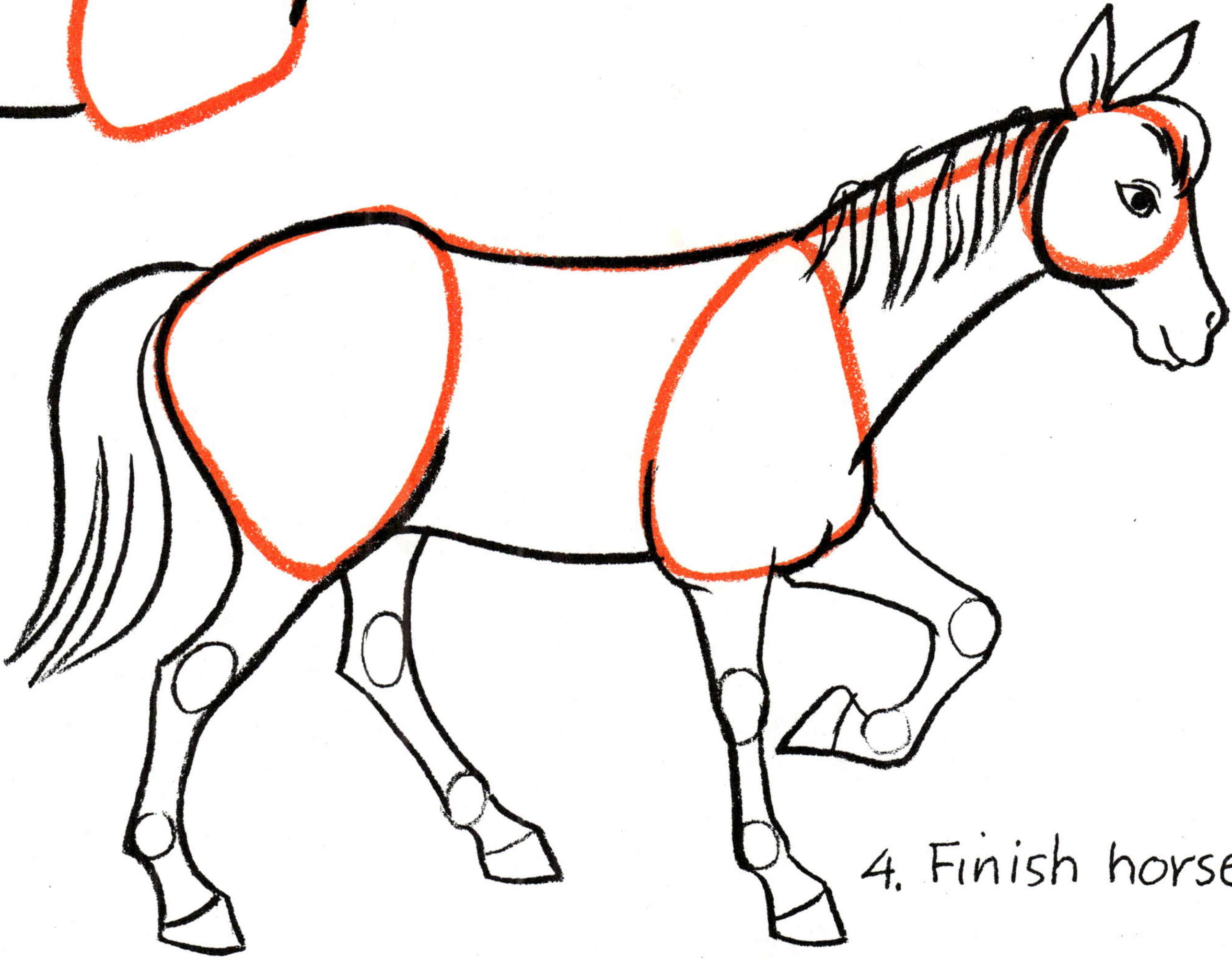

4. Finish horse.

Raccoon

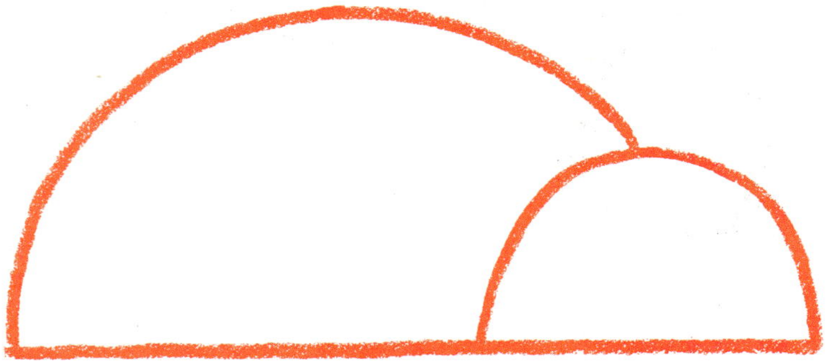

1. Draw two half circles.

2. Add eye shapes, ears, nose and hands.

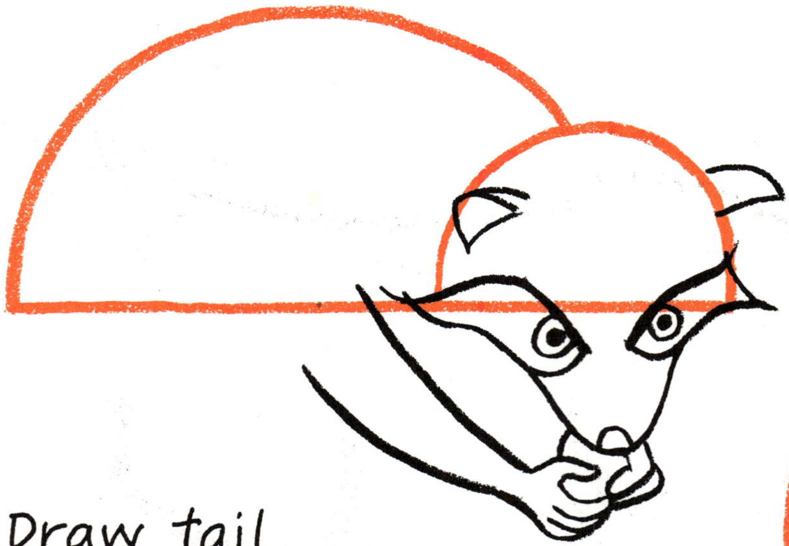

3. Draw tail, rear leg, and finish head.

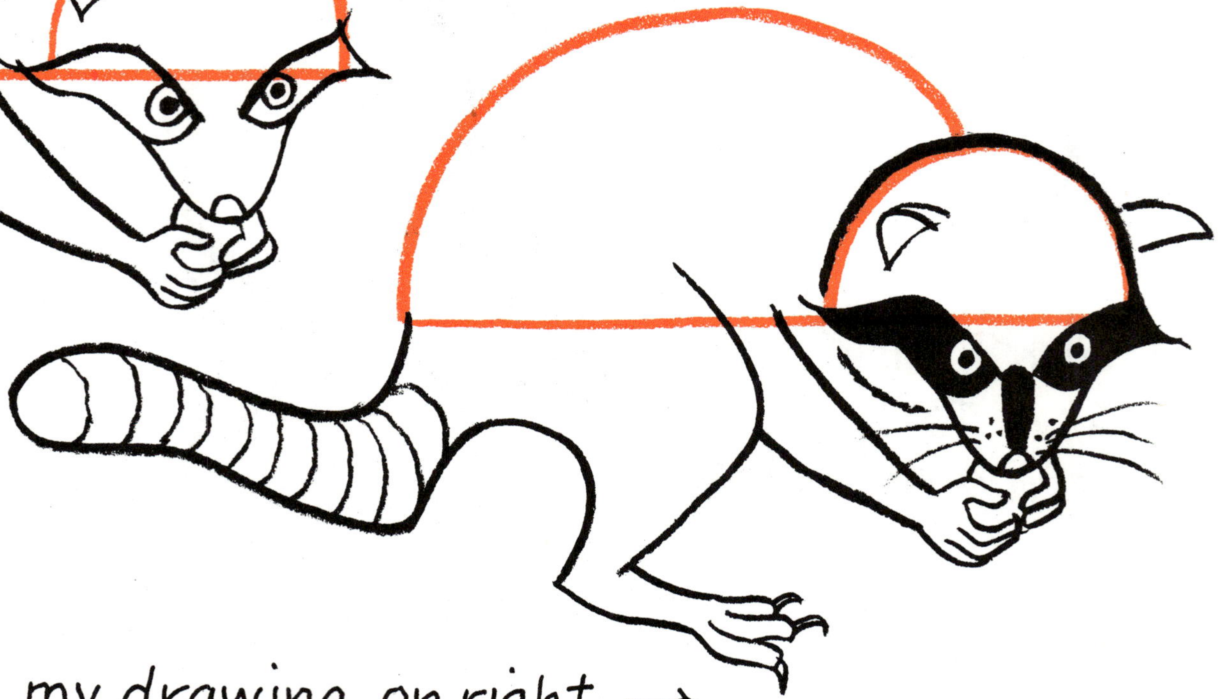

Complete like my drawing on right →

I made this raccoon drawing in a Natural History Museum.

Try drawing from nature, or from animal pictures in magazines, books or photographs. Pick out the simple shapes first.

The Disney Studios encouraged their artists to sketch outdoors in zoos, parks, beaches, etc. We were to simplify the drawings, and get a feel for movement and action. This is easier if you can picture the shapes in motion, then add details later.

Remember, first find the simple shapes!

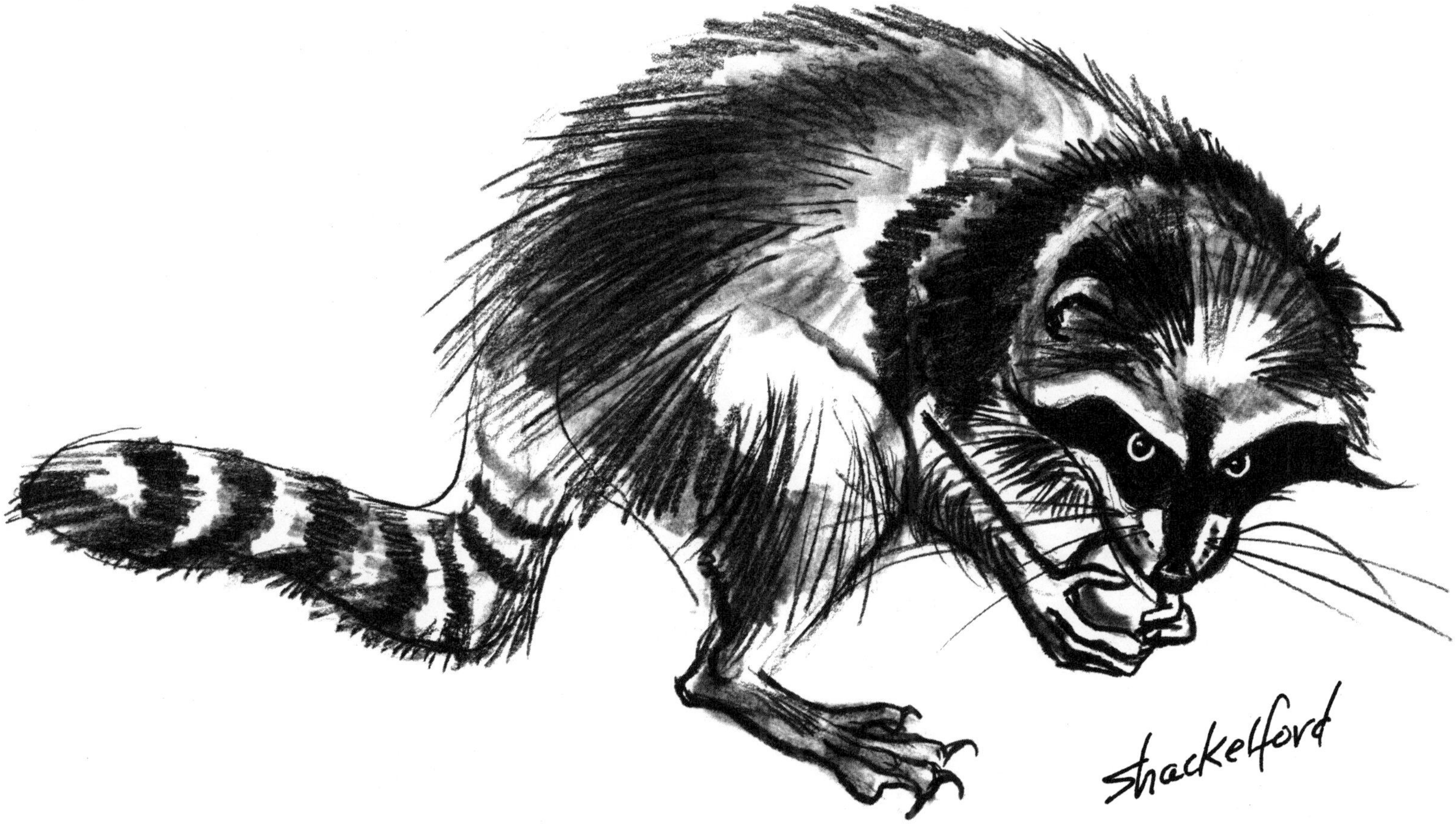